REA

ALLEN COUNTY PUBLIC LIBRARY

3 1833 04266 3937

S0-BVN-361

TRANSFORMING
OUR TERROR

JUL 1 8 2002

OTHER BOOKS BY CHRISTOPHER TITMUSS

Spirit for Change

Freedom of the Spirit

Fire Dance and Other Poems

The Profound and the Profane

The Green Buddha

Light on Enlightenment

The Power of Meditation

The Little Box of Inner Calm

An Awakened Life

The Buddha's Book of Daily Meditations

Buddhist Wisdom for Daily Living

For further information about books, tapes, and retreats, contact:

Gaia House, West Ogwell, near Newton Abbot, Devon TQ12, England

Tel 44 (0) 1626 333613

email: generalenquiries@gaiahouse.co.uk

website: www.insightmeditation.org

www.gaiahouse.co.uk

www.dharmanetwork.org

TRANSFORMING
OUR TERROR

a spiritual approach to making
sense of senseless tragedy

Christopher Titmuss

BARRON'S

Terrible grief and distress can explode upon our lives at any time.

The behavior and action of others may cause us unimaginable pain,

or we may bring such pain upon others or ourselves through careless

action or deliberate intention. We have a responsibility to work

together toward transforming deeply distressing events in our lives

for the peace of mind and security of all. The intention behind this

book is to explore ways to resolve suffering, regardless of the

circumstances in which it arises. My deepest sympathies go out to

those who have to endure living through hell regardless of

background or nationality. May all beings live in an awakened life.

CHRISTOPHER TITMUSS

First edition for the United States, its territories and dependencies,
and Canada published in 2002 by Barron's Educational Series, Inc.

© 2002 Godsfield Press
Text © 2002 Christopher Titmuss

Produced exclusively for Barron's Educational Series, Inc. by Godsfield Press.
Designed for Godsfield Press by The Bridgewater Book Company.

Illustrator *Sarah Young*

All rights reserved. No part of this publication may be reproduced,
stored in a retrieval system, or transmitted in any form or by any means,
electronic, mechanical, photocopying, recording, or otherwise.

All inquiries should be addressed to:
Barron's Educational Series, Inc.
250 Wireless Boulevard
Hauppauge, NY 11788
http://www.barronseduc.com

Christopher Titmuss asserts the moral right to be
identified as the author of this work.

Library of Congress Catalog Card No. 2001097842
International Standard Book No. 0-7641-2221-5

Printed and bound in the U.S.A.

9 8 7 6 5 4 3 2 1

CONTENTS

In August, I managed to secure the last available seat on a Virgin Atlantic flight from London to San Francisco for Tuesday, September 11, 2001.

 THE PREVIOUS WEEKEND, a friend in The Netherlands had kindly driven me to the village of Westerbork where, about sixty years ago, the Nazi army ordered more than 100,000 Dutch Jews into a transit camp. After days, weeks, or months in the camp, the Jews were loaded onto cattle trucks bound for Poland and the concentration camps. I had wanted to visit Westerbork because of a book I had been reading and rereading for years. It was the Amsterdam diary and letters written from Westerbork by a twenty-seven-year-old Jewish woman named Etty Hillesum, who remained obstinately determined to live out her life with passion, reflection, and freedom. Etty's resilience and moral fiber in the face of uncertainty, danger, and death had always inspired me.

On the packed flight to San Francisco, I renewed my connection with Etty by reading an edition of her book combining her diaries and letters. I was particularly struck by a passage in which Etty described her reaction to an interview with an arrogant Gestapo officer, who had tried to frighten her by threatening "to see her later." Etty wrote that the Gestapo was "more afraid of us [the Jews] than we need to be afraid of them." Her words made clear that she had faced her personal fear to the point that the Nazis held no terror for her. The occupying army on her doorstep might deprive Etty of her conventional freedom, but no outer event could compromise the freedom of her spirit. My absorption in the book was suddenly interrupted when, five hours into the flight and not long before we would enter U.S. airspace, the pilot announced via the intercom that we were turning back to London. "All airports in the United States are closed due to terrorism," he said. "That is all the information that we can give you at the present time."

Meanwhile, back home, my twenty-year-old daughter Nshoma had switched on the television and seen news of the highjacking and crashing of four passenger flights, including one bound for San Francisco. She knew I was flying that morning to San Francisco, but not with which airline. The report sent her into a spiral of alarm and tears. It took more than two hours for her to confirm that I was on a Virgin Atlantic flight even then on its way back to London. Nshoma's anxious uncertainty pales into insignificance when compared with the trauma and despair of tens of thousands of people who lost loved ones that day. In Nshoma's case, the reassuring voice of a member of the airline staff dispelled her distress. Yet, the same voice could have reported something quite different. For each of us at every moment, relief or bereavement rests on a word.

As we journey through life, we hatch various plans, dream of ways we might improve our situation, form hopes and visions. The real world of dramatic and unexpected events mostly passes us by, as though the daily news belonged to another realm unconnected to our personal concerns. It is as if we cannot afford to let our consciousness expand beyond the field of the known and familiar.

Sometimes, it seems, we can barely watch a traumatic moment in a movie, let alone deal with events in the real world outside. We may have thought about something unexpected happening—an automobile accident; a house fire; a devastating storm or earthquake—and speculated about how we might cope with it. Yet we sense that nothing can prepare us for the shock and terror of an inconceivable event exploding into our everyday existence. We seem barely equipped for dealing with tragedy.

But in every life, it seems, circumstances arise with such a savage degree of unpredictability that life is turned upside down, its pieces scattered in a horrifying way. Unbidden, terror comes into our lives through past and present events and through our fears about what might happen in the future.

In the nightmare of such catastrophe, the inner life tries to make sense of what has happened, seeking some way to come to grips with the collapse of the foundations of our existence. Violence, abuse, rage, exploitation, withdrawal, and bereavement have the potential to ignite a sequence of reactions that can lock us into a psychological prison charged with anxiety.

What can help us at such times? This book explores the process of coping with sudden disaster, drawing upon wisdom, ancient and contemporary, from Buddhism, Christianity, Judaism, and Islam, that aims to help us comprehend the incomprehensible. It has three goals:

The first purpose of the book is to explore a spiritual approach to making sense of any senseless tragedy or horrific event. It suggests that we may have to realize that learning to live with unanswerable questions is better than finding comforting answers. As an example of this process, it draws on recent international events, particularly the deep divide between the West and the Islamic world that symbolizes for our time how fragmentation between cultures generates mutual fear and mistrust. When we experience a similar divide in our personal relationships, we often stereotype others, both individuals and societies. Such reactions inhibit our ability to be aware of the whole picture, without the blinders caused by divisive feelings, perceptions, and memories.

The second purpose is to explore our emotional life as we deal with terror, sadness, sorrow, despair, anger, hatred, and the desire for retaliation. It suggests ways we might transform terrible experiences so that they become the basis for a fresh way of looking at existence. It is a central teaching in this book that we cannot transform others, or ourselves, through inflicting pain upon those who have harmed us. It argues that a retaliatory mindset always bedevils authentic and lasting change.

The third purpose of the book is to shed light on a transcendent understanding of recent events, such that, through knowing ourselves, we simultaneously come to know others. It invites us to transform recent world events into the opportunity to realize, perhaps for the first time, that we have more in common with each other than what separates us. We each have the capacity to embrace life in its fullness, both the beauty and the horror. Through reflection and soul-searching, we can discover in terrible happenings a perspective that affects us to the core of our being.

It is my hope that this examination of recent events will change how you view the predictable and unpredictable experiences of life. It invites you to shift beyond the simplistic and often unexamined beliefs that color your perceptions. When you do, you stop hiding behind labels of good and evil and work to overcome the negative conditioning that hardens deluded perceptions into the desire for retaliation. Instead, you address the causes and conditions that trigger terror. You see that answers to the profound issues of life are found outside the storyline of typical conclusions about personal or international catastrophe.

If we can learn from recent history, we won't be doomed to repeat it—either to bring despair or to heap blame upon others or ourselves. Etty Hillesum and others like her remind us of the extraordinary power of the human spirit to transcend fear and flourish in the face of catastrophe. We, too, can become inspirations to others if we have the courage and determination to transform our terror into understanding and wisdom. This, I believe, is the only way forward.

Christopher Titmuss
Devon, England

REFLECTIONS AND MEDITATIONS

At the end of each chapter, there are exercises, reflections/meditations to help transform terror in some of the various ways it reveals itself. There are some basic principles to bear in mind for reflection and meditation.

• Find a quiet time, either at home, outdoors or in a quiet place, such as a religious building.

• Sit with a straight back, either in a chair or cross-legged on the floor.

• Take a few, conscious breaths allowing the mind and body to relax.

• Slowly and gently read (out loud, if you wish) each of the statements or questions. Remember to take your time. Let each phrase or sentence sink deep within. Let the truth touch the heart.

In the case of those exercises in the form of questions., listen to any inner responses, observe any reactions, and notice any appreciation in your response. If a phrase or theme strikes a chord, go back to it. Consider its application as a resource for daily living. For some people one particular practice or meditation may be an important cornerstone of their daily life for years ahead.

CHAPTER ONE

Working with Grief

Let not a person revive the past

Or on the future build his hopes

For the past has been left behind

And the future has not been reached

Instead with insight let him see

Each presently arisen state.

Let him know that and be sure of that.

Invincibly, unshakeably.

The Buddha
Middle Length Discourses 131

 TERRIBLE EVENTS, SUCH as those of September 11, 2001, in New York, Pennsylvania, and Washington, and their aftermath have the capacity to affect people in radical but different ways. How we react to such catastrophes depends to a large extent on our inner spiritual resources. Three very different stories of those caught up in the events of September 11 and their aftermath can provide insights into the range of responses in the face of terrible tragedy.

PETE AND MICKY: FIREFIGHTERS' STORIES

Pete, a New York firefighter from the 29th Street Station, reported (*The Observer*, UK, October 21, 2001): "Three days after it, I was an emotional wreck. I'd cry at the drop of a hat. I came back to work three or four days later. That was the best therapy, the chance to dig a little bit. It's hard being in a station where we lost so many guys. I was talking to every one of them that morning, drinking coffee, discussing what we'd have for lunch. They get a run, and it's like OK, see you guys later. Then, that's it. They're gone. It could easily have been me."

Micky, another firefighter from the same station, said: "I guess I was stuck inside the building two or three hours. I remember the first time I looked at my watch it was 2 o'clock. It's amazing the watch survived except for the damned plastic band, which broke. Suddenly, I don't know how they found us, but there were a couple of people above us. They had made it down. They set up a guide rope. When I was in the hole I said if I ever get out of here—which I didn't think I would—I would never set foot in a firehouse again. But I've decided to give it a few months. My original plan, prior to September 11, was to retire a year from now, because I will have done 25 years. Now all I want to do is to take one day at a time. I don't wanna make a decision that will affect the rest of my life based on what happened to me [on September 11].

"It may sound odd, but this whole thing's created a certain feeling in me now that I don't feel any obligations to anything or anybody. I feel in a sense free, like I can do what I wanna do. I no longer feel so bound up with things, with things I think I have to do. I don't have anything to do now. I feel like I'm free to live a day at a time. I see how life is, how short it is."

THE RODRIGUEZ FAMILY

In New York, the parents of Greg Rodriguez, one of the young men who died in the Twin Towers of the World Trade Center, said: "We read enough of the news to sense that our government is heading in the direction of violent revenge, with the prospect of sons, daughters, parents, and friends in distant lands dying, suffering, and nursing further grievances against us. It is not the way to go—not in our son's name."

The Rodriguez family express one of the most profound of human feelings, namely empathy. They have realized that their sorrow and the sorrow of others are no different. That understanding allowed Greg's parents to express to journalists, family members, and friends their concern for others in another part of the world.

THE AHMED FAMILY

The family of Gul Ahmed—husband, wife, and seven young children— lived together in a suburb of Kabul. Mostly unaware of the terror around them, the children played with each other, laughing and teasing as children love to do. Then the bombs came. Ahmed's wife survived the bomb attack, but her husband and all seven children died. "Why are they not taking any decisions to stop this?" the sorrowing mother asked a reporter. "Why are they doing this to us? What have we done to deserve this?"

Both Mr. and Mrs. Rodriguez and Mrs. Ahmed had much in common than what separated them. They had lost their nearest and dearest, and neither family could find any explanation for such a devastating loss. Both felt that terrible anguish within. Both asked: "Why? Why? Why?" It is the willingness to acknowledge the shared depths of human suffering that brings people together.

The range of emotional responses, from the simple grief as experienced by Pete and the sense of dislocation and loss of direction felt by Micky, to the generous forgiveness and concern for others expressed by the Rodriguez family, and the complete disbelief and incomprehension of the mother of the Ahmed family, clearly indicates how varied our response to terrible events can be. Many people experience a wide spectrum of emotions over the course of their grieving, moving between feelings of anger, vengefulness, self-pity, and despair as they search for a way of coming to terms with events. In the wake of tragedy, we need to consider how we can help others and ourselves through this process and learn how to cultivate a spiritual wisdom that will help us to transform grief and suffering into inner peace.

THE INITIAL RESPONSE: FACING THE TRUTH

One day we live utterly enthralled with our personal relationships or work, and the next day we have been exposed to a devastating shift of events that plays havoc with our sense of security. Where do we turn? Can we make sense of the senseless? Do we need to? Is there some kind of understanding beneath the inexplicable anguish of events?

A few years ago I was asked to meet with a man, aged about 45 years, whose 19-year-old son had died the previous month in a motorcycle accident. The father had brought up his son on his own with an extraordinary degree of love and devotion. They lived together in a modest apartment and, with the passage of years, had developed a deep bond with each other. The loss of his only child broke this man's heart. When he walked over to meet with me, his whole demeanor reflected the weight of his pain.

In the midst of sorrow and grief, there is a strong voice of resistance that cannot bear to accept the basic harsh truth. The deep ache and the anguish fight the bare facts. There is often a denial, even hatred, toward such information and the descriptive circumstances that surround it. "No. No. It can't be true," were the first words that the loving father used when the police told him his son was dead. There is a struggle within between one inner voice that knows the truth and the other inner voices that refuse to accept it. This terrible inability to come to terms with events tormented the father day and night.

As a first step toward healing, we have to find the ability to open up to and absorb the truth, accept it, and stay with it. Such prescriptive advice is easy to say, easy to write down, but not at all easy to put into practice. It is hard to make the transition from "no" to "yes" without reservation, from denial to acceptance without resistance, so that we can stay steady with the truth of things. We might even interpret any protracted denial as some kind of proof of our love for another rather than a blocking out of that love, due to the waves of sorrow and the resistance to change. Would the person who has gone from our life wish to bestow such grief as the final legacy of their relationship with us?

The sadness that permeates our hearts due to the arising of the unwelcome, the unwanted, and the unforeseen has a certain weight that can bear down upon us until we feel sick to our stomachs. Our chests contract and our heads feel stuffed full of unpleasant sensations. The overall pressure releases tears out of our eyes as the breathtakingly painful information begins to sink deeper and deeper into our hearts. It is not easy, but when we begin to relax and accept, to breathe fluidly, we find ourselves reconnecting with the world around us. We can listen to the words of others. We can feel the warmth of their sensitive concerns and touch. We start to take our first tentative steps toward the renewal of our spirit. Our lives are not lived in isolation, but through our relationship with others, near and far, as much as with ourselves. Renewal and healing start to take place when we rediscover the capacity to make contact and form healthy relationships with others.

REJECTION AND THE DESIRE FOR REVENGE

As humans we share the earth and live in contact with each other in a variety of ways. In the era of high-tech communications we are interrelated to the point that we can make an impact on each other's lives without ever even meeting each other. The world has truly become a global village, in which we can serve as a great support for one another or support decisions to inflict terrible suffering upon one another.

When others hurt us, directly or indirectly, we need to deal with our responses or reactions to this feeling. The feeling of being hurt by another easily presses numerous emotional buttons. Unable to cope with feeling hurt, our reactions can escalate. We feel hurt, then upset, then irritated, angry, enraged, and perhaps then determined to get some form of revenge or support others to act upon our behalf. Through a variety of rationalizations, our minds justify their desire for retaliation, cloaking the emotional response through systematic thought and action to take steps to express revenge.

Despite the rhetoric to justify our desire to inflict pain on others, when we go down this path we are failing to appreciate that, at the emotional level, we cannot find a way of handling these feelings of hurt other than with a negative reaction. It is the great task of truly thoughtful people to try to understand these emotional pains, hurts, and wounds, and to transform them so that we can emerge with a greater insight that enables us to develop a nondestructive approach to resolving the deep rifts that exist between people.

In response to hurt, some people react against themselves, producing a range of distressing inner emotions where sorrow and guilt implode upon each other, causing despair. When we feel fear and horror, we may hate life and hate ourselves. This hastens our withdrawal from others, and our retraction into a shell to protect ourselves from the world and from our own pain. This helplessness easily leads to more despair or the determination to exact revenge on another.

From a spiritual standpoint, we need to listen to the voice of the parents of Greg Rodriguez. Like many others, they had to endure enormous suffering yet they refuse to give support to retaliation. Beneath the pain and anguish, there is a depth of goodness and purity wishing to protect others from having to suffer in a similar way. There is something that we might call noble and dignified about such thoughtful and compassionate viewpoints despite the loss of their son.

SELF-BLAME AND GUILT

Sometimes we blame ourselves for having allowed something awful to happen to those around us. In such cases, a small event can loom large in our minds when it appears to be the cause of a very painful result. It is understandable that whenever we experience a painful consequence to events we seek to name the cause and how we deal with it. Riddled with guilt and self-hatred, we become racked with torment, in a kind of war with ourselves. It is a difficult but important task to see the bare facts of the situation free from the personal investment of the self.

On that fateful day in September 2001, one of the staff in the Twin Towers felt unwell at home and had decided to take the day off. Her partner got angry with her and persuaded her to go to work rather than stay at home. He took the view that his partner was not as unwell as she claimed. She reluctantly went off to work. Two hours later she was dead.

Her surviving partner felt not only grief at the closure of a long relationship but terrible guilt for having persuaded her to go to work and for not listening to her. Instead of holding the terrorists responsible for their crimes, he started blaming himself. Inwardly, he kept grasping onto his final conversation with his partner, thus making himself the primary cause for her death instead of acknowledging numerous conditions forming together.

The experience of guilt and the perception of causes bear a close relationship. At times of deep levels of emotional pain, it is hard to see clearly the differences between a primary cause and other factors. This leaves individuals vulnerable to waves of guilt and remorse until they find some degree of peace within.

Similarly, some survivors of catastrophe experience guilt as well as sorrow, grief, and despair for the death of others. They seem to blame themselves for having survived. In the most extreme cases, this can result in a loss of the will to live due to the intensity of guilt. It becomes vitally important to develop an attitude that acknowledges the range of our emotional reactions rather than perceiving them as a statement or reality about ourselves. We pay respect to those who have departed from this world through love, gratitude, and appreciation, not through guilt and despair.

Opening ourselves up to others around us must take priority. Feeling their love and natural empathy works to dissolve the wretched sense of helplessness and misery. When those who have gone through a great trauma set out on the road to recovery, they remain vulnerable to tender memories, which now become acutely painful. There is a danger of them slipping backward; but significant contact and association with others whom they trust can sustain the potential for inner empowerment and help dispel isolation, despair, and helplessness. Day by day, with this support, they consciously leave the past behind.

COUNTERING DESPAIR

If we are unhappy, and not experiencing a fulfilled relationship with existence, then, whether we know it or not, there is an underlying pattern of general dissatisfaction influencing our daily lives. A violent attack, tragedy, unwanted loss, painful change, or bereavement intensifies the pre-existing anguish until it becomes overwhelming. The distress that naturally results from unforeseen catastrophic events may have an even more devastating impact if it adds to an accumulation of sadness.

We feel that our whole world is falling apart, that nothing could be as bad as this situation. Overwhelmed with grief and despair, we may experience no light, no hope, and no reason to continue living. In extreme cases, we magnify the problems of daily life to the point where we seem to be going from one crisis to another. In some circumstances, despair is an understandable response.

Patience is vital. It takes enormous vigilance and determination to keep remembering that the waves of emotion and the intensification of views get wrapped up together, inciting each other to a painful intensity. Although it will be a long, dark night, it will pass. Every acknowledgment of change we give ourselves or receive from others matters. Patience and steadfast reminders of the impermanence of all these experiences will support the process of becoming calm and the understanding of events. This will sustain a long-term recovery.

LONG-TERM RECOVERY

Although many people find that tranquilizers, sleeping tablets, and antidepressants help in the immediate aftermath of a traumatic event, such measures lack the capacity to bring about long-term emotional healing. Nor is time the answer. Unresolved issues will continue to linger in corners of the heart. We have to explore our inner resources to be able to move on with our current lives, which never stand still, not even for a moment. If we do not do this, we will remain trapped in the past instead of waking up to the new day and new beginnings.

THE VALUE OF SUPPORTIVE FRIENDSHIP

In the traumatic state caused by the loss of a loved one, friends and family of the suffering person may experience a sense of helplessness. Some may take the view that there is nothing they can do to help the person going through this distress. "They have to figure it out for themselves" or "They need time" become typical responses. Some will say, "I don't call. I don't know what to say," or "Whatever I say doesn't seem to be the right thing." It is easy to forget the importance of pure presence, where we share silence, show patience, and, if necessary, encourage the person to seek emotional or religious counseling or help them go about everyday matters.

It is the sign of a good friend that we offer friendship to others struggling to cope with unexpected changes affecting their lives for years to come. We can carry on being a good friend without being overbearing and without avoiding the painful issue. Even embracing all these qualities, the relationship with a person in recovery from suffering will not be easy.

Difficulties arise that test our trust and confidence. Painful memories and unresolved dependency issues easily become transferred onto the friend, the sympathetic family member, or the counselor. It is no easy task to give support to a person going through a grief process. There is the deepest wish to help, but feelings of inadequacy and doubt can arise when trying to help somebody through a huge loss.

I have learned not to offer advice but to ask questions, to allow the individual to talk, to share feelings about a painful chain of events. One question has to bear a connection with the last question so that there is a natural flow. Those who grieve need to feel heard, to feel listened to, and especially to feel understood. We do not need to know what to say, but we need to sense what we should ask.

FINDING THE RIGHT WORDS

Terrifying experiences cause us to feel fear and mistrust, and it becomes all too easy to transfer these emotions onto others. We suspect that nobody can understand what we have gone through, that nobody really knows how to listen or respond with the right words. It is not unusual for someone in deep pain to say, "You don't understand." It takes a certain quiet inner strength to hear all this without feeling hurt or giving up listening to the narrative of pain. It is a pity if a family member or good friend underestimates the importance of maintaining contact with someone facing an emotional crisis.

People express their deepest feelings about life through various means, including religion, a practical philosophy, or a faith in life or themselves. A devastating shock can play havoc with all these views. Previous hurt and disappointment easily give rise to further sadness, and we can develop a cynical view about life. The intensity of such views can alarm the listener struggling to come to terms with the person's pain.

What matters may lie outside of language, beyond words, and be present in a dimension of silence, of sacred spaces, the sense of communion and nature. The troubled individual can keep repeating the story of terror to the same person or various people without finding any inner peace, or finding release from the experience. It can become a form of identity that the individual is reluctant to drop. The story may stay much the same or it may change, it may be congruent with the facts or it may not, it may be part factual and part imagined.

It takes patience to remain sensitive and respectful in a way that shows a compassionate awareness to those who pass through an intense struggle where feelings, thoughts, memories, and events meet together to form a distressingly painful picture.

TRANSFORMING GRIEF AND RESTORING HAPPINESS

At first glance, the issue of happiness seems to bear very little relevance to the sadness that permeates our hearts due to the arising of the unwelcome, the unwanted, and the unforeseen. However, if we are to think about how to restore happiness following the trauma of a terrible event we need to develop our understanding of the nature of happiness and emotional well-being.

As human beings on this earth, we are basically gentle, resilient creatures when we live at peace with ourselves and in harmony with events. This means we are usually able to come to terms with what life brings us. However, this capacity is severely undermined if we live in an inner world charged with unsatisfactory influences from the past, out of touch with natural happiness on a daily basis, and alienated from the realities of living one day at a time. If we perceive life as simply a means to satisfy personal desire, then we run the risk of experiencing an utter inability to cope with circumstances that work against the demands of the self.

Intellectually we cannot fathom the reasons for deep happiness. There is a limitation to the mind's capacity to comprehend joyful matters of the heart and the intensification of exquisite feelings. Moreover, if we move into our minds—our mental framework of concepts and intellectualization—we experience a diminishing of that volcanic upsurge of joy as consciousness moves from heart to head.

Even after a catastrophic event, the restoration of happiness is affected by our life values and priorities. If we neglect our friends and the outdoors, our capacity to relax and experience natural enjoyment will be subsequently diminished.

It is never easy to establish such priorities in our daily lives after moving through a hellish state of existence. But every effort we make in this direction will be rewarding. We feel better not only about ourselves but about others and about life itself.

There are many reports of the restoration of happiness in people's lives through their capacity to initiate fresh priorities that offer the possibility of opening up to a whole new perspective. This movement away from the unsatisfactory grip of the old into a new and more caring view toward all of existence is the mark of a spiritual person.

SHIFTING PERSPECTIVE

It is no coincidence that survivors of life-threatening situations, who have walked the thin line between life and death, report a dramatic shift in their perceptions. The sheer intensity of the drama dissolves the notion of continuity and makes a mockery of attempts to plan life, possessions, and goals.

The self-created priorities fade into the background so that the fullness of life itself has the opportunity to break through into consciousness. The realization of the significance of living one day at a time provides the foundation and groundwork for a different way of living that is free from all the usual preoccupations, obsessions, and fantasies.

Micky, the New York firefighter whose experience was described earlier in this chapter, reported that he realized he really had nothing to do. His words mirror and reflect ancient spiritual teachings which say that, in life there is nowhere to go, nothing to do, and that this moment is it.

To imagine that something else is better, different, or worthwhile misses the freedom, the great liberation available, when our existence and the present live grounded together in a harmonious fusion.

In order to maintain inner peace of mind, it is essential to try to adopt the role of witness rather than becoming a participant. The true witness is not passive, but attempts to take an overview and maintains a sense of caring responsibility for the totality of the event, free from bias.

It is not uncommon in religious texts to speak of the importance of "witnessing," but this usually refers to people of a particular faith who give testimony to their beliefs. In spiritual teachings, the witness has a vital role to play in bringing awareness and insight to the resolution of suffering; in bringing "heaven," that is peace and reconciliation, to a potentially hellish situation. Detached and unbiased, the witness seeks to diffuse suffering, to dissolve the climate of negativity, and to see an end to the strife and the stress that accompany it.

Through witnessing and connecting with life, rather than living in pursuit of what we want, it becomes self-evident that the strength of our suffering depends upon the relationship we have with our past, present, and future. Instead of escaping from the here and now, we must try to embrace it, take a deep interest in its expression, inquire into it, and apply mindfulness to the ordinary events of life. Through sudden insight or gradual understanding, we can dissolve the problems around our relationship to this world and ourselves. Sages have always reminded us of the timeless discoveries available when we are willing to let go of clinging and attachment to what we cannot have, future fantasies, and indulgence in memories—so that the power of now can register its impact upon our consciousness, uninhibited by our likes and dislikes.

The true witness to life develops a naturally transcendent viewpoint that is free from conditioned thoughts and ideas that obscure the pure immediacy of things and their liberating impact. We need to take note of the profound words of Micky, expressing the freedom he feels about living one day at a time. When we express such a feeling there is little opportunity for the ego to create an identity out of the streams of thoughts, or our personal storyline. We lose the appetite to measure our existence through the ownership of consumer goods, or through roles and social status. In a liberated consciousness, the things that we previously craved or secured become meaningless. There is a different dimension to life that bears no limits, no restrictions. We go about our daily business free from the constant ego gratification that snatches temporary, pleasurable sensations and resists unpleasant ones.

Our capacity to witness and truly live for today, with all its various aspects, offers a depth of peace and contentment that is unavailable to the mind that frets over past, present, and future. In this inner peace, our tendency to attack others or to pursue transient success loses its grip over our lives. This is a sane way of living in this world that keeps us directly in touch with daily life, beyond the desperate clinging to a one-sided view and the ignorance of others.

A CARING, SPIRITUAL APPROACH

In conflict, far too many people take a hard-hearted view of the death and suffering of the innocent in times of war. They forget the pain and tears brought upon men, women, and children who play no part in international conflict. A spiritual awareness calls upon us to listen to the concerned voice within, rather than the hard voice that says: "These things happen in the time of war. What do you expect?" The appeal of the Rodriguez family for political restraint and the questions of Mrs. Ahmed, born out of the depth of her grief, deserve our attention so we can find ways to respond with a caring heart rather than with declarations of war. It is not only an emotional shift but also a shift in consciousness, a shift in intelligence, to soften the hard voice within to a wise response. Society has much to learn in the area of resolving human conflict.

Peace and harmony are often dismissed as abstract concepts suitable only for those who uphold a romantic view of life. Through our own experience of grief, we can realize the transforming power of the here and now and its benefits for a sane and compassionate way of existence. Terms such as "being with God" or "realizing enlightenment" take on a depth of meaning and become immediate and accessible to us. The enlightened words of some survivors of tragic situations remind us all to stay in contact with the present—as the anchor of existence.

An example of how the experience of catastrophe can be transformed into practical, constructive action is provided by two men working to clear the deadly land mines that were the legacy of a past war in Afghanistan. They spent the day working inch by inch, step by step, to make it safe for the villagers to go to the fields to plant their seeds. Every morning they got up and went back to the place they had finished the day before. Children from the village watched them from a safe distance. Every time they uncovered a mine the children would clap and cheer and run and tell their parents. Such brave men inspire us to take positive steps, to move forward to bring peace of mind into this world.

Trained in the West, these brave men go into the fields and along dangerous tracks to make areas safe for people they do not know or even have the capacity to speak with because of the differences of language. The dedication of such men and women to the welfare of others represents countless expressions of compassion, a true sign of a spiritual awareness. There are men and women working for many organizations around the world whose primary concern is to uplift the lives of others. Perhaps some would not call their work "spiritual," but their support for strangers and their work on behalf of strangers show that these workers are the true gods and goddesses of the Earth.

In the face of adversity the commitment to stay steady with the flow of life, with the support of others, enables us to journey toward a full recovery. Then we will discover natural happiness as well as the capacity to deal with any future traumatic events that might affect our lives. This natural happiness springs from wisdom and clarity about the world we live in. There is something profound and beautiful about bringing a spiritual awareness to the intense dramas that arise in life. We may be a minority voice, but it is voice that reminds others of the importance of awareness, love, and deep respect for existence.

DEALING WITH PAINFUL CIRCUMSTANCES

If you are experiencing upsetting or traumatic events—or you are in contact with someone who is—read through the following suggestions and try out a few at a time.

1. Remember to breathe mindfully in and out. Taking several long, deep breaths helps to take the power out of painful thoughts and memories.

2. Keep the channels open for communication with others. This includes inviting loved ones into your home, going out, making use of the telephone, sending e-mails and letters. As much as possible, keep appointments. Remember that others mean well, even if they seem to say the wrong thing.

3. Write down your feelings honestly without censoring what you write. This may include keeping a diary or writing down on pieces of paper what you are going through. You may prefer to use a tape recorder to record your thoughts and feelings and the steps you are taking to come to terms with events.

4. Spend time outdoors or sit at a window as often as possible. There is a certain healing power in letting natural light in through the eyes. Such a daily practice helps to keep us grounded in the present and connected to the world around us, as well as providing moments of appreciation of natural beauty.

5. Refuse to indulge in painful memories. The pain of the past and feeling sorry for yourself in the present intensify despair. It is probably true that letting go of memories, including painful ones, is the hardest thing of all. Yet, it is an important principle for moving on from painful events.

6. Stretch the body in various ways throughout the day or attempt gentle exercise. If you feel very unhappy, your energy levels slump, and your posture may become heavy and contracted. Regular physical activity, such as taking long walks or practicing yoga to bend and stretch the body, helps you to recover energy and assists the struggle against despair.

7. Make a commitment to take one day at a time. The further your mind wanders into the past or future, the greater the likelihood of hurt, disappointment, and fear. Practice taking one day at a time so that you don't become overwhelmed with images of the past or anxieties about the future.

CULTIVATING AN EXPANSIVE OUTLOOK

Our outlook on events matters a great deal, both in the short and long term. There are various ways that we expand our outlook so that we can arrive at fresh insights in attending to situations, whether personal, social, or political.

1. Reflect on the benefits of what is present in your life. Even in the midst of great hardship, we can find blessings, although it may be terribly dark and full of foreboding at the time. The human spirit has an extraordinary capacity to work with intolerable situations.

2. Try to cultivate various disciplines in daily life that reflect wisdom and careful thought. These include speaking from personal experience rather than from hearsay and not feeding the inner voices of ignorance, prejudice, and reactivity. By adopting these modes of thought you will uncover fresh ways of working through anguish.

3. Acknowledge how desire for more puts you out of touch with immediate existence. If we lack appreciation for what is present in our life, we keep trying to fill a void within. This void disappears when we develop and cultivate an expansive sense of connection with the world we live in

4. Spend time in touch with the natural world, free from ownership and possession. If we spend more time in nature and less time, for example, in shopping malls and looking up websites, we experience a significant change for the better within. Contact with sun, clouds, trees, flowers, and water nourishes human existence and promotes joy and peace of mind.

5. Cultivate kindness toward others, whether loved ones, strangers, or those who are unfriendly. Kindness is a powerful force when directed to all without exception. It keeps the heart open to fresh ways of transforming difficult situations between people, whether people whom we know or people who live in other societies.

6. Offer service. Volunteer to help others who are suffering and to know first-hand their experiences. This can help to dispel opinions that result from lack of direct knowledge of what we are talking about.

7. Draw on the wisdom of others. Spiritual and moral exemplars can provide us all with a great deal of inspiration when events burden our daily lives.

HELPING OTHERS THROUGH THEIR PAIN

Our concern and support for those who are grieving can make an immense difference. It is never easy, but there are several important points to bear in mind when we make ourselves available for one who is in pain. We need to remember to:

1. Ask questions that allow the grieving person to talk freely about their feelings.

2. Pay attention to what they are saying without being judgmental.

3. Be aware and accept that we may become temporary targets for transferred anger of the person who is grieving.

4. Remain sensitive and respectful, being supportive without being overbearing or trying to force the pace of the grieving process.

5. Recognize that we may feel the need to withdraw from the supportive role from time to time.

CHAPTER TWO

Dealing with Negativity and Conflict

Love your enemies.

Do good to those who hate you.

Bless those who curse you.

Pray for those who mistreat you.

Do to others as you would have them do to you.

Jesus of Nazareth
Luke 6: 27, 28, 31

WE COME INTO contact with conflict and negative actions in many different aspects of our lives: home, workplace, neighborhood, and in the wider world. The following stories illustrate three types of conflict.

JULIE AND HER FAMILY

Julie, a teenager, lived with her mother and stepfather in a household where yelling and swearing at each other about issues such as staying out late were the norm. The stepfather mostly stayed in the background, though he backed his partner in her arguments with her daughter. One day emotions reached such a pitch that the mother slapped Julie across the face and evicted her from the family home. Julie went to live with friends.

In her efforts to justify her act of retaliation, the mother sought and gained the support of her friends. Similarly, the daughter spoke with her college friends, telling them that she could not understand how her mother could treat her in such a way. Her friends sympathized with her. Neither would apologize and neither would take responsibility for her inflamed attitude. The mother said, "My daughter and I are at war with each other. There seems to be no way out."

After a long period of silent animosity between mother and daughter, Julie telephoned her mother to try to break the frozen atmosphere between them. Initially both mother and daughter could not communicate on the telephone. One or the other would slam down the phone as the heat of their disagreement grew. It took a mutual friend of both mother and daughter to start bridging the wide gulf between parent and child. The friend, a neighbor, explained the position of the mother to the daughter and vice versa. The mother then softened her attitude and made space again in her heart for her daughter.

A STREET ATTACK

Walking home late at night from a friend's, a foreign student crossed the street to avoid a gang of youths walking on the same side of the road. He knew better than to walk near the gang at such a late hour. Swearing and shouting, the gang accused him of avoiding them. They then chased him along the street, eventually catching him. They beat him up and kicked him, breaking his teeth, fracturing his ribs, and hurling racial abuse at him. After the beating, the gang left him bleeding and wounded while they continued swearing and cursing at the student's presence in the country.

Luckily a passing motorist spotted the nearly unconscious young man lying in a pool of blood on the sidewalk. He called the police and an ambulance. It took weeks for the student to recover. Asked about the incident later, the victim expressed no rage toward those who persecuted him. "I feel sorry for them," he said. "They were looking for someone to take out their hatred upon. They picked on me. Their lives must feel very empty."

The family that the young man stayed with wondered how he could be so forgiving. The young man had no particular religious beliefs or philosophy to guide him. He told the family that he realized that the gang's projections of rage upon him had nothing to do with him. He knew he was an innocent party. "If I get angry with these violent men, it means I have sunk to their level," he said. Despite face wounds, cuts, numerous bruises, and a black eye, he explained: "I cannot take it personally. There are some very angry people around. I was in the wrong place at the wrong time. Anything can happen when people are under the influence of anger and prejudice."

NETA AND THE SOLDIER

In January 2002, I received an e-mail from an Israeli friend who works tirelessly in the occupied West Bank for justice and reconciliation. Neta wrote that she had spent the day planting trees with the villagers of Deir Istiya. She was on her way home when two soldiers recognized her. Neta described her conversation with the soldiers.

At one point one of the soldiers told her, "When I see a terrorist lying on the ground in his own blood it gives me an appetite." He hesitated before continuing. He wanted to reveal something he was proud of. "There was a time when someone in Hares village picked up a huge boulder to throw at me. Do you know what I did?" he asked.

Remembering the incident, Neta said "You killed him. Let me tell you who you killed."

"I don't care," responded the young soldier.

"I know you don't, but I want you to know who you killed. His name was Muhammad Daud, a 15-year-old retarded boy whom I loved very much." She told him everything she could think of about Muhammad and about his family. The soldier did not want to hear it. She wrote, "His resistance was the only indication that maybe somewhere deep inside there is a piece of humanity still intact. I realized that the soldier I had just spoken to was an ignorant boy who should never have been given a rifle."

DIFFERENCES AND CONFLICT

Every conflict reminds us of the strength of differences that can exist between people, including loved ones. Individuals, groups, or nations can maintain their particular fixed viewpoint until it leads to aggression and violence. It then becomes an enormous challenge to make an inner shift to exploring constructive ways to resolve the force of negativity from another.

The three stories told above illustrate conflicts caused by intransigence and failure to see another point of view, prejudice against those who are different, and violence caused by fear and an inability to appreciate fully the consequences of actions. In each case, resolution occurred because one party had either the wisdom to question a previous fixed position (as in the case of Julie and her family) or to refuse to let a negative action create a similarly negative response (as in the case of the injured student). In the case of the young soldier, Neta's understanding of the soldier's fear and immaturity allowed her to escape anger and bitterness about his role in the death of her friend.

Deep spiritual teachings remind us to endeavor to rise above such situations so that we do not respond with hatred when subjected to hatred.

These approaches help to bring about a depth of heartfelt awareness so that we understand that the violence of others arises because of ignorance, unresolved inner pressures, and a mind darkened by forces of negativity. Those who inflict violence upon others remain trapped in their situation as much as a prisoner in the basement cell of a prison.

The first step to avoid becoming involved in an ever-escalating cycle of damaging responses and to bring about a peaceful resolution of our differences is to explore ways of countering conflict and negativity. If we can contemplate on the similarities of the human condition when facing rage and conflict, whether in personal life or political situations, we may start taking further steps toward resolving problems without recourse to intensifying conflict through what we say or do. As with the brave young Israeli woman, it takes a spiritual approach to find a resolution through the willingness to listen, the ability to speak up, and acts of reconciliation.

To transform negativity into understanding requires a depth of honesty with ourselves, a determination to question whether self-interest is at the expense of another, and a frank admission that the sequence of feelings of helplessness, frustration, and desire for retaliation is painful and ultimately unfruitful for all concerned. If we truly admit this to ourselves, then we have begun the process of meaningful change that will help us uncover and realize alternatives that echo profound spiritual teachings on love, forgiveness, and inner transformation.

THE RESPONSE TO ATTACK

You have been attacked, robbed, violated, harassed, or bereft of the love of your life. You may be on the receiving end of the intolerance or rage of another, even though you may have no wish to be party to such a conflict. You are frightened by the impulsive reactions of somebody you know. You are afraid to travel to a certain location, terrified by an aggressive neighbor, or overwhelmed by the demands of some current situation in your life. When you face frightening and disturbing events, you often wonder what to do, or doubt that you have what it takes to handle these demons.

As the pressure and pain expands, your anguish can reach such a pitch that you close out the world, blocking the senses. Have you wondered why you cannot bear to listen to a well-meaning voice in those first hours when the full weight of circumstances descends upon you? Although you might want the presence of sympathetic friends around you, their words often sound like platitudes and the experiences they try to share seem to pale by comparison with your grief. When we are faced with such conditions, we often feel utterly isolated from all that is beautiful and sacred in life. Although others assure us that the situation will improve, we barely allow ourselves to hope.

We often feel overpowered by conflict. There may be a sense of impotence in terms of handling a difficult, if not threatening event. Rather than appear passive, an angry person may be subject to an overwhelming desire to impose a particular end on another. Hatred and retaliation may be disguised as punishment when the reaction originates from a frightened state of mind that is compounded by a sense of helplessness and frustration. Whether the conflict is personal, social, or political, we need to cultivate an awareness in ourselves of these responses, which may be expressed in behavior and actions that create suffering for others. The outcome of such deep resentment may explode in a single moment or sustain itself through decades.

Yet, if we can avoid spiraling into despair, like the student in the story of the street attack above, we can find the inner strength to get through such dark times. The young man showed a remarkable degree of maturity in his attitude toward his attackers. He saw no point in getting into a rage over their actions, appreciating that by doing this he would only sink to their level. Without his determination to understand those who attacked him, the young student might have fallen into such despair that he would have become unable to live a normal life following the incident. He might even have blamed himself for being in the wrong place at the wrong time. We need to focus our attention not only on coping with our personal pain but on seeking to understand the forces that have generated it. In this example, the childhood upbringing of the young man's attackers, as well as their social environment, unresolved personal issues, alcohol, violent projections, and an inability to accept responsibility for their actions were all major factors. Difficult circumstances reach far into our lives, leaving us little alternative except to come to a deep sense of acceptance of the conditions that make us, and those around us, act as we do.

WITNESSING CONFLICT AND NEGATIVITY

When we are exposed to an event our eyes and ears register what is happening. We may see a tragedy on the television, witness it directly with our own eyes, read about it in a newspaper, or hear about it from another. Whether you comprehend it or not, this immediate contact has the capacity to set in its wake a series of responses or reactions that reveal much about ourselves and our view of others. The contact generates an impression that passes through the doors of our senses into the depths of our inner lives.

The strength and description of the story, or event accompanying the contact, influence our inner response. Clearly, that inner response varies according to personality. For some people the most terrifying events bring a mere shrug of the shoulders. Others will experience a tremendous shock, breaking down into tears, their whole body visibly shaking. There is no objective response because people deal with their impressions of events in various ways, but true witnessing is a good response.

A true witness connects with life and applies mindfulness to it, bringing awareness and insight to the resolution of suffering. The following story provides an illustration of effective witnessing. Outside a bar in Darwin, Australia, a fight began between a group of men with broken glasses and bottles. The scene terrified some people, while others crossed the road, not wanting to get involved. Two young women, who appeared to be the partners of two of the men fighting, broke down on the pavement in tears screaming "Somebody do something, somebody do something." Several minutes went by before the police arrived.

During this time, one middle-aged woman went up to the group of fighting men and spoke quietly and gently to them. It was such a shock to them that they stopped fighting and started yelling and swearing at her to make her leave. The woman was fearless, not taking a single step back or raising her voice. She just kept talking. Waving their fists at each other, the men stormed off in different directions. She witnessed. She acted. She refused to take sides. She dissolved a fight. Others who were standing around watching the melee broke into a round of applause. The woman said nothing and continued her journey home.

We have no idea what the brave woman experienced inside as she confronted those involved in the fight. But she clearly did not allow any inner terror to stop her from expressing her concern. It is one thing to appreciate such courage, but it is more important that we practice taking forward steps, even though we may tremble within when facing a confrontational situation.

THE REACTION TO PAIN AND FEAR

Much can take place after an initial contact with a painful or frightening situation that causes feelings to arise faster than the blink of an eye. One momentary contact can produce an immediate reaction when pain is felt. Take a very simple domestic example. After cooking food in the oven, if we forget to hold the cloth properly, our bare fingers make brief contact with the tray inside the stove. The pain registers and suddenly, out of the blue, we utter a curse word, even though we never use such a word in our everyday vocabulary. We then slam the oven door as a reaction. A moment of painful contact acts as the condition for subsequent events.

In some situations, such as burning your fingers, there is little likelihood of a negative reaction continuing after the initial incident. However, a painful situation can sometimes make an impact that affects behavior long into the future. If a child is bitten by a dog, it is possible that the fear of dogs will continue into adulthood. If someone has offended us in the past, we may still hold a grudge years later.

If we fail to examine our reactions to events, we can easily become locked into a pattern of reaction that we repeat indiscriminately with every painful experience. This pattern shapes our way of dealing with whatever happens to us. We need to learn to reorient our consciousness so that the past is clearly acknowledged as the past, and the present and future offer the potential for change. It may require a thousand reminders for this to register to the degree that it makes a difference, but if we do not work to make this shift, it will mean that we will needlessly continue to suffer the pain of past experiences, thus sustaining unhappiness and inflexibility.

We need to remember that all experiences of the world around us are filtered through our state of mind. In other words, we can to a great extent choose how we react to what has happened. We can make a lot of something, a little of it, nothing of it, or somewhere in between, according to the condition of our inner lives. A transcendent view does not dismiss events or our contact with them, but simply keeps a vigilant awareness over this contact and warns us if our reactions are leading to hostility or other negative responses. This helps to dissolve the tendency to vengefulness or despair that can dominate subsequent perceptions, and we can then act wisely.

AWARENESS OF FEELINGS AND STATES OF MIND

There are three primary categories of feelings and motivations that contribute to negative states of mind: the pursuit of desire (our own wants and ambitions); rejection and revenge seeking; and neutrality and nonengagement. Authentic knowledge about others or ourselves requires an understanding and awareness of all three types of feelings and subsequent states of mind, since they are the primary influences on human behavior.

We can start by tracking in ourselves what happens after an initial contact with a problem or conflict and by assessing the outcome. Is our response motivated by a narrow pursuit of self-interest, by rejection and the desire to hurt, or is it governed by indifference or avoidance?

Feelings arise from an initial contact such as a sight or sound that may be pleasant, unpleasant, or somewhere in between. In a single hour, we find ourselves exposed to countless impressions we hardly register, while other contacts give rise to feelings that make a big impact on our consciousness. As the mind enters the field of feelings, whether pleasant or unpleasant, we have the opportunity to perceive what these feelings and impressions are about. This allows us to produce a range of thoughts and reactions to these feelings. Unpleasant feelings can easily stir up negative memories from the past, and long-held impressions can contribute to a proliferation of negative views of past, present, and future events. This combination of feelings and memories may saturate our consciousness and distort our perception of present events to the extent that we are unable to separate the true information from our reactions to it.

Even though the initial intensity of a past reaction has long since faded, a basic set of opinions remains in the mind that only serves to support our preconceived opinions. We cling to these opinions because past events have once hurt us or made us feel angry. We then resurrect an inner picture of those events that sums up what we imagine was the true reality of what took place instead of acknowledging that memory and negativity have become fused together to create a warped picture.

As this view crystallizes in our minds, it generates further attachment to this viewpoint, leading to arrogance, disputes, and accusations against others. When we hold onto a reactive view of events in this way, we are inwardly blinded and can tolerate no other viewpoint. The mind shrinks around the view, defending it from criticism and becoming intolerant of others' perceptions.

However, circumstances can change, and one day our truth may change and become a different truth. We protect the truth when we acknowledge that our view of a situation is simply that—our view. If we do not cling to our view, it allows for other responses to become available, free from reactivity, despite the continuity of many of the same feelings. To know ourselves is to know that this process is at work and then we are able to witness what stage of the process we are experiencing. If we fail to look at ourselves, then we are liable to move from an unpleasant feeling to an inflamed reaction, followed by aggression.

A conservative religious man was very proud of his lawyer son and loved him deeply. One day his son came to him and told him that he was gay. The man was very shocked and could not bring himself to speak to his son for two months. He had always held homosexuality to be morally wrong. However, knowing his son to be a good man, he was able to reconsider his view and ultimately achieved a shift in his opinion. The father and son were reconciled. Such responses may occur within groups as well as in individuals. Every year we read in newspapers of political groups and religious cults that develop a culture of narrow exclusivity around a set of beliefs. Such groups may end up causing terror for others, and society may respond in like toward the group.

If we know that our response is unwise and unhealthy, then we need to make a commitment to transforming our whole attitude. The various reflections, meditations, and exercises in this book offer practices for achieving inner change, a fresh perception, and vision to work with any major issue, no matter how overwhelming it seems at the time. With inner understanding, we can safeguard ourselves from sinking deep into the swamp of unhappiness and thoughtless reactions. Otherwise, faced with a frightening situation, our inner lives can enter a destructive spiral of negative reactions that burns up all that is good and beautiful within.

THE NEGATIVE FORCE OF DESIRE

Suffering arises in life through what is existing or through what is not existing, through what is present or through what is not present. Existence and nonexistence—whether of material or nonmaterial things—become intertwined with the process from contact through to feelings, thoughts, and desires. If we are unable to accept presence or absence, then the force of desire—the pursuit of our own agenda—can gain enough strength to initiate an action that deliberately causes suffering to others. In cases of conflict with another person, when this mind-set is present, tension and pressures can build up to the extent that we experience the constant desire to censure the other person, and may even verbally or physically attack the other person. Years later, if we have not addressed our negative feelings, we may still try to justify our past actions, failing to comprehend such divisive views or the harm they have done to others.

Without the impartial witness, the dark force of aggressive desire forces us to be preoccupied with what is existing and its painful continuity, desire for something to continue, or desire to get rid of what is existing. Wisdom involves the skillful handling of issues of presence and absence as well as changes, great or small.

In the story of Julie and her mother, recounted at the start of this chapter, we can see how each of them stubbornly pursued her desire for control in the relationship, contributing to a complete rift. In this case Julie was eventually able to change her viewpoint to act as an impartial witness to the build up of rage and retaliation, and so released a shift in perspective within herself and then from her mother. The one who first makes the shift expresses a greater degree of emotional maturity.

In increasing our spiritual awareness, we have to learn to observe the strength of desire, arrogance, and rigid standpoints within ourselves so that we understand such feelings as forces that produce the need for retribution. Spiritual wisdom cannot develop while the ego (selfish desire) dominates our thinking, so we must learn to take a step back from this egotism to take the power out of it.

DEALING WITH TERROR IN THE WORLD AROUND US

Major catastrophic events, especially those that are caused by human action, have enormous and lasting impacts that tear into the fabric of society. We have to investigate new ways of dealing with such situations and learn to respond to the power of a spiritual perspective that seeks reconciliation rather than retaliation. In the ancient Chinese text, the *Tao Te Ching*, the sage Lao Tzu wrote: "Give evil nothing to oppose and it will disappear by itself." This principle applies to both personal and international situations.

To examine this widespread arena of painful experience, we have to engage in soul-searching, which can be extraordinarily difficult. We resist it and may find it hard to avoid the desire for retaliation and the inflicting of pain on others in response to the pain inflicted on us or those around us. As we get close to taking an honest look at ourselves, we will probably keep coming up with questions such as, "What about them?" At this point we need to examine the way we keep reinforcing the belief in "us and them." This is very difficult. Tragic events can either reinforce even further the "us and them" syndrome with its painful consequences, or they can provide the inspiration to unpack this division and perceive things in another way.

We need to see that violence, whether undertaken in an "official war" or as a terrorist act, creates pain and suffering to others. If we feel somewhere deep within ourselves that blame and its intensification into retaliation only recycles painful consequences, we are forced to examine our responses to such political solutions as waging war to stop war.

In the Eastern traditions this cycle is referred to as karma. Strictly speaking, it refers to the unsatisfactory influences of the past upon the present. When these influences go unexamined, we experience the painful fruit of the karma. It is the examination of karma that leads to its transformation and the end of the painful cycle of problems and suffering. Insight and wisdom dissolve the cycle of karma.

With this understanding, we then have to explore a different kind of relationship from those who want to impose their wrath upon others. That intention marks the start of a spiritual search to uncover a new approach to coexistence. In a celebrated talk, Jesus told his listeners to "turn the other cheek" in the face of hurt. This means to look in a fresh direction for our response to the violent actions of another, a much more active approach than the more usual interpretation of this philosophy—the blind acquiescence to anger and violence.

At times, we need to be reminded of the words of Mahatma Gandhi, the great Indian nonviolent activist against the injustice of British colonial rule in India, who said that if we adopt the eye-for-an-eye view of justice then it will make the whole world blind. In other words, our capacity to turn the other cheek shows that we are neither afraid of an adversary, nor are submitting to him, but that we have the strength of mind to respond in an utterly different way to what an adversary expects. In Eastern terms, our capacity to show initiative, courage, and vision means that we have broken the old karma, namely reaction leading to reaction, hatred producing hatred.

THE TRANSFORMATION OF CONFLICT

Whether through acts of war, a tragic collision of circumstances, or upheavals in the forces of nature, we live a vulnerable existence without any assurance for tomorrow, no matter how much satisfaction or success today brings. However, when others deliberately inflict pain upon us, we easily treat like with like. Do we really want to do this? This is the core issue that needs to be addressed if we are to resolve conflict in fresh ways.

When terrible events occur in the world around us, we usually have little choice but to get on with our lives, continuing to do all the necessary small things that make up our existence. For some of us international tension may increase normal worries about what the future may hold to a high level of anxiety. What will our leaders do next? What will those who hate us plot next? Why do things go so terribly wrong? Why do so many innocent people have to suffer? What can we do? We have to learn to live with questions that seem unanswerable in the present or near future. These questions may never leave us.

Throughout history humankind has constantly re-created the dualistic pattern of "us and them." "Them" reinforces "us," and "us" reinforces "them." We fail to realize our common humanity and instead the self declares war on the self. It sometimes seems that international conflict has become a private matter between competing political and military forces trying in every conceivable way to assert control over a situation through destroying the perceived threat. We are left with a mixed message: that nothing will be the same again and yet nothing must change.

Honest reflection and soul-searching bring people throughout the world closer together so that we realize we have more in common than what separates us. We have to learn to think differently about and to connect with one another through a power that is not a military one.

If we stand back from a situation and refuse to take sides where one side endeavors to inflict suffering on the other, we have the possibility of achieving a different kind of awareness—one that is not colored by emotion, latent prejudices, and long-standing reactive thinking.

How do we find a different way of looking? How do we witness what is happening without taking sides? What does it mean to look beyond conditioned loyalties? What leads us to believe and accept a particular version of reality? What leads us to reject another version opposed to our view? In such questioning, we must remember the value of the non-attached witness who is willing to explore ways and means to resolve conflict and must not be afraid to doubt the versions of reality that filter through our media.

The task of the witness is to dig deep, to go beyond a fragmented view in order to realize a holistic view. In this way, it is possible to dissolve the intensity of the enmity and friction in opposing standpoints and move decisively toward constructive engagement. We have the capacity to experience empathy with those who are suffering, and this constitutes the initial awakening of a deeply spiritual approach to conflict.

Although it is not simple to achieve, the authentic spiritual life cares passionately for those who suffer while remaining willing to examine dispassionately the conditions and causes that produce such suffering. The Buddha declared repeatedly that he only taught two things: "There is suffering in this world. There is the resolution of suffering in this world." He protested about the use of force to resolve conflict:

When someone kills people, he is murderous, he has blood on his hands, given to blows and violence, is merciless, then unwholesome states of mind increase and wholesome states of mind decrease. So he abstains from wounding, murdering, plunder and violence, he abandons the killing of people and puts aside his weapons.

Human behavior is often contradictory—we may work to resolve personal suffering while simultaneously heaping blame and denunciations on others. This gives us some self-satisfaction, but changes nothing. We have to find out for ourselves about the conditions that allow suffering to arise and the conditions for its cessation, rather than live in a vindictive and malevolent manner. The witness looks into the nature of suffering, sees the fixation of perceived differences, and endeavors to reveal a new way of understanding that ceases to perpetuate the divisions. We have to show courage and explore the alternatives. The Buddha said that compassionate action then takes priority to transform the cycle of suffering.

RESOLVING CONFLICT

In the following section seven important areas that contribute to resolving conflict are outlined for consideration. I believe they are applicable to any situation, whether in our personal lives or in the wider arena of intense conflict between communities or nations. Conflict in the home or workplace can often be avoided if you remember that everyone is entitled to a point of view.

1. Explain the value of your attempt to resolve the problem to all the various parties without making it a confrontation. This means showing that your initiative acknowledges the other party's needs as well as your own. The suggestions need to be practical, concrete, and genuinely helpful.

2. Endeavor to understand the other party, no matter how difficult it seems. You may need to encourage them to clarify the issues that concern them so that any resolution feels practical and workable for both parties.

3. Endeavor to find a facilitator or third party who is clearly free from prejudice to mediate. If either party feels stuck in their differences, unable to find common ground to serve each other's interest, then the skills of the nonattached witness who can facilitate procedures are invaluable. A forum, whether at the personal or political level, may become necessary.

4. Do not get caught up in the attack–defend syndrome, because it is a destructive cycle. Each party may feel they are right and the other is unreasonable or inflexible (see *Julie and Her Family*, page 25). In the heat of the moment, intolerant and aggressive statements can be made that risk triggering a similar response from the other party.

5. Treat the other party's position as a viewpoint, an option they advocate, without attacking it. Undertake inner work, such as meditation, before and during an intense meeting to help you stay calm, cool, and considerate—no matter what is heard.

6. Regard your position as an option that is open for others to question. There should be no absolutism in communication but a growing capacity to see a point of view as a point of view. It is not only what we say that is important. The tone and attitude are equally significant.

7. Treat attacks, no matter how hurtful or destructive, as expressing a desire to resolve the problem. Sometimes one party may launch into a bitter tirade against the other. It may seem unfair and unjust, but the person making the attack is expressing, albeit unskillfully, a wish to resolve the problem.

MEDITATION ON LOVE TOWARD THREE KINDS OF PEOPLE

Practice these meditations regularly for all three kinds of people. At times, you will need to concentrate on a particular group due to circumstances. As you speak the lines, remember to bring in the feeling of the heart to go with the words. It can be worthwhile memorizing the lines or similar lines to enable a loving presence to be steady in the heart whenever we are in contact with others.

(This meditation is taken from the author's book *Buddhist Wisdom for Daily Living*.)

TO LOVED ONES

• May I always acknowledge and understand your intentions.
• May I always be supportive for you in time of need.
• May I never place demands and pressure on you.
• May you be well and happy.
• May your life know contentment and joy.
• May you be peaceful and steady from one day to the next.
• May our love and friendship for each other remain steady.

TO STRANGERS

• May I not rush to judgment on meeting you.
• May I show friendship and presence for you.
• May I communicate clearly and wisely in your presence.
• May your day be rich and worthwhile.
• May you act mindfully and consciously in all things.
• May everybody treat you with respect.
• May you show kindness to everybody that you meet.
• May your day be free from fear and worry.
• May you sleep well and peacefully tonight.

TO THE UNFRIENDLY

• May your bitterness and resentment subside quickly.
• May you understand the pain you cause yourself and others.
• May you explore fresh ways to explore differences.
• May you see into the fear behind the anger.
• May you develop equanimity when things do not go your way.
• May others stop being angry toward you.
• May you realize that anger does not cease with anger.
• May others listen to you and you listen to others.

CHAPTER THREE

Overcoming
Fear and Anger

Words of Wisdom spoken softly

make much more sense

than the shouts of a ruler to a crowd of fools.

Wisdom is more powerful than weapons.

Ecclesiastes 9:17

 AT FIRST GLANCE, fear and anger may appear to be quite different emotions. However, the two emotions bear a close relationship, each feeding off the other. Fear invites anger, and anger creates fear. You may have witnessed how a dog whimpering with fear in the corner when threatened by another dog may suddenly turn and attack the aggressor, forcing the other dog to retreat or to become even more aggressive. Such rapid switching between fear and anger also commonly occurs in human interactions, but this cycle can be transformed.

THE NATURE OF FEAR

Fear is a kind of mental desperation that we experience when we come into contact with events or the actions of others that seem to threaten our security or safety. The impact of such events may be to shake and disturb us from the depths of our beings. In many cases memory of past episodes of fear combines with new information so that our feelings escalate to the point where we feel that we cannot handle things any more. There may seem to be no point in continuing, since the very fabric of our existence may seem to be at risk.

Plummeted into this frightening chaos, we may struggle through sleepless nights and disorderly days, attempting to keep ourselves above the inner torment that other people can sense is within us but do not feel themselves. This is hell. There is no other word that describes this condition more aptly; no experience is comparable to the nightmare that seems at the time as if it will go on forever.

In the midst of such emotional turmoil, it is almost impossible to make any sense of what is happening. However, after the initial trauma has subsided, it is vital to be aware of the impressions you have been left with, because this emotional residue will determine future feelings and thoughts. Is the residual impression a fear? Or is it courage? Is it anger? Or is it kindness or clarity? While the memory of the tumultuous state of the emotions may fade, they may continue to have an impact on our lives through the residue that remains in the heart. It is a little bit like a stain in a valued tablecloth. Focusing on the stain, we may conclude that the whole tablecloth is ruined. However, although we may initially feel sad that something has been spoiled, we should realize that circumstances can change. Just as the tablecloth may be restored by repeated washing, so our residual impressions can be altered by continual soul-searching.

If we fail to acknowledge what is happening, these waves of reaction to painful events will continue to surface from the depths of our being, like volcanic eruptions, giving us no time to enter any state of recovery. Each new crisis threatens to blow apart our carefully constructed worlds. Nothing feels right, nothing feels valid, and the notion that there is some purpose to existence seems truly perverse.

For some, fear can lead to an extreme level of emotional imprisonment. In such cases there are lessons to be learned about taking one step at a time, as the following story reminds all of us.

After three years of enforced confinement in a psychiatric hospital, a homeless young man was told that he could leave the hospital. However, the distressed patient felt afraid to leave the security of the fifth-floor ward, resisting all efforts to go downstairs to the main entrance to his freedom.

A psychiatric nurse took the patient under his wing to help him overcome his fears. The nurse made a simple agreement with the young man. He asked him to take one short step every day. The nurse drew a line with chalk on the floor where the last step finished. The following day the young man would take a step from that chalk line.

Over weeks, the young man made his way down through five floors to the main entrance. The nurse had successfully supported his transition into the world by helping his patient gradually overcome his fear of letting go of all that he had—namely life in the ward of a psychiatric hospital. We can ask too much of ourselves if we think we can overcome every fear in a flash.

Anticipating various situations can challenge our capacity to stay steady and lead to the emotion we know as fear. The main categories of fear are fear of losing what we have (including fear of loss of health or life); fear of what other people think or say about us; and fear of experiencing mental pain. The old adage that to be forewarned is to be forearmed certainly applies with fear. We have a duty to work with the little fears that beset our daily life in order to develop and mature as human beings. If we ignore everyday fears, then we will lack the capacity to handle our biggest fears when we are forced to confront them, and this failure may plunge us into depression or the pursuit of retaliation.

FEAR OF LOSING WHAT WE HAVE

The widespread preoccupation with having and owning is in fact a form of desire fueled by the fear of not having and not owning. It sometimes seems that the more we have, and the more expensive the goods, the more we fear their loss. At some point it becomes debatable whether the pleasure of ownership outweighs the fear of loss.

However, fear of loss is not exclusive to affluent societies; it can happen to anybody anywhere on this earth at any time. Sometimes the level of suffering for the very poor seems to reach a greater pitch than for the wealthy and privileged. If you possess nothing except a family to love and care for and a mud hut with one or two utensils for cooking and farming, you invest all your feelings, your hopes, and fears into these few things you have. It is heartbreaking to lose them all or to have them threatened, no matter what the circumstances. Life becomes a struggle to deal with what fate hands out and a continuous effort to cope with all the associated fears. Negative events, whether local, national, or international, whether expressed through violence, sickness, natural disasters, or loss of livelihood, bring a depth of despair and grief to the poor that the affluent can avoid through access to medication, professional help, insurance, travel, or through emotional escapes through television and work.

Privileged and underprivileged alike are also subject to fear of losing their loved ones. It is never easy to cope with our changing, unreliable existence where there is no guarantee of continuity of existence or of sustainable security in relationship to others.

If we have trouble coping with these harsh facts of life, then our inner world experiences insecurity, sometimes manifesting itself as fear and anger over the uncontrollable flow of life. The Bible reminds us that everything has its time and its season, including birth and death, planting and reaping, laughing and crying, embracing and parting, finding and losing, love and hate, war and peace.

FEAR OF WHAT OTHER PEOPLE THINK OR SAY ABOUT US

If we travel through daily life haunted by the need for approval and the fear of disapproval, it produces within us a constant need to justify ourselves and to make ourselves acceptable and agreeable to the perceptions of others. Such efforts not only take the joy out of life but also leave us vulnerable to having blame, faultfinding, and negativity foisted upon us. It seems to make no difference whether we regard ourselves as blameless, blameworthy, a bit of both, or simply misunderstood. Ultimately, whether other people's opinions reflect the truth is of little relevance to those who live in fear of what is said about them. If we transcend our fear of others' opinions about us, we gain the inner strength to stay steady with the truth of things regardless of what other people believe.

Desires, images, feelings, and thoughts consolidate to support the underlying tendency to want to be liked, to be loved, and to be appreciated. The desire for such attention, and the demands that often go with it, only succeed in deterring true friendship, creating further self-doubt. For some, the subtle body language or words of others determines whether a day is good or miserable. When we have granted such authority to others over our state of mind, our existence is superficial, and the deep virtues that nourish a worthwhile existence are ignored.

The emptiness of an existence in thrall to the approval of others is highlighted by the experience of a French film star: "Millions of men around the world adore me, but I only want one man to truly love me." She told a reporter that she spent many lonely nights consuming a cocktail of drugs and alcohol and with her pillow soaked in tears.

Although overconcern for the opinions of others can be damaging, we nevertheless need to assess honestly the impact we make upon others. Some people seem not to care at all what others think of them. They believe their own self-created story that they can do what they like regardless of others' views. Indulging in the dubious pleasure of notoriety, they pursue actions to secure attention, including hostile attention, from others. In this way they also expose their dependence upon what others think of them, whether this is expressed as approval or disapproval. Unable to be in contact with their inner needs, nor understand their workings, these self-cherishing individuals find themselves consumed with both negative and positive thoughts that are never resolved.

With this type of attitude, "Everybody else is wrong and I am right" may become our maxim when the words and actions of others make an impact on our lives. Desire for approval and resistance to disapproval become two sides of the same coin. We have given authority to others to push and pull our minds around rather than to respond to the voice of wisdom, whether inner or external. We allow others to determine our peace of mind or lack of it, rather than explore a change of heart from reaction to insight, from hostility to constructive engagement, from revenge to working toward understanding.

Public figures who have made every effort to be as pleasing to as many people as possible often find themselves living in a world where their peace of mind revolves around praise and blame, no matter how hard-nosed they claim to be. In particular, ambitious and self-serving politicians and celebrities are often afraid to express publicly their deeper concerns and values, and instead they make insincere statements that are congruent with millions of others. In the name of popularity they may endorse ugly features deeply embedded in the national character, such as making war to solve conflict. When our political leaders tell us they have no choice, in a sense they are right. It is a very rare human being who has the freedom to make a compassionate choice while in political office.

FEAR OF EXPERIENCING MENTAL PAIN

Have you ever made a serious mistake during the course of your life? Have you ever acted in a way that is less than perfect? Have you ever done something that you now consider irresponsible, arrogant, or simply deceptive? What were your reactions? What did you go through? What were your feelings and thoughts afterward?

There are two judges in daily life: one operates from without; and one springs up from within, often acting as judge, jury, prosecutor, defense, and sentencing authority. Some people judge themselves through a severe inner critic that surges into their consciousness, through faultfinding, self blame, and self-condemnation based on what they have done or have failed to do. It is a malicious form of self-torture, which obscures rather than brings clarity to our thoughts. Such self-loathing gives no assurance that personal history will not repeat itself.

Countless numbers live in fear of their own state of mind. Because of their low self-esteem, they lack both the inner and the outer resources to transform their perceptions, and they stumble through each day never sure whether they can handle the problems that inevitably arise. This low level of self-confidence brings hesitation and stops us from resolving issues inwardly. We need to transcend negative states of mind, including guilt, shame, and self rejection, which cloud our clarity of mind and prevent us from giving our full attention to resolving difficulties. The Buddha said that nobody could do us as much harm as our own ill-directed minds. With resolve, we have the opportunity to make it absolutely clear to ourselves that the past is the past, and be sure in very specific ways what we have learned from past mistakes. We need to ask ourselves the following questions: What specifically shows the differences between our present understanding and that in the past? Is there need for some kind of atonement? If so, what action might express it: reparation; genuine apology; asking for forgiveness; or some form of spiritual commitment?

Years ago, I stayed in the hill station of Dharamsala in the foothills of the Himalayas in India, where the Tibetan community now reside after they fled the military occupation of their kingdom by the Chinese. One day, I made my way down a winding footpath through the fir trees that stand above Mcleod Ganj, a village nestling above Dharamsala. In a converted cow shed, I met with an aged and wrinkled Tibetan. His hut was empty except for a worn-out mattress on the floor, a couple of blankets, and one or two items of clothing on a hook. He kept a rusty cooking stove with a kettle and a saucepan. A single unframed photograph of the Dalai Lama hung on the wall above his bed.

Beside the bed there lay a long wooden board that the Buddhists from the Himalayan countries, especially the Tibetans, use for their full-length prostrations, performed from the standing position. I have been to India about 30 times and on many occasions have witnessed Tibetans, as well as a number of Westerners, engaging in the spiritual discipline of making prostrations while simultaneously saying a mantra.

In that cold Himalayan room, I noticed that the board had deep grooves in the hard wood in the places where his toes and fingers rested when his body was at full stretch. I pointed to the marks. He said that it was due to the number of prostrations he had made. He explained that following the Chinese invasion he had fought and killed Chinese soldiers. In today's language, some would call him a "freedom fighter."

"I felt very bad," he told me. "After all, they were the sons of somebody else's mother and father. I had caused much suffering. I had made very bad karma for myself. I did not know how I could ever repay the karmic debt that I owed. I decided to embark on these prostrations." I asked him how many he intended to do. He replied: "I have made a vow to make five million prostrations. I will not stop until I have completed this vow. I have to make an atonement for what I did."

"What if you feel the karma is not exhausted?"

"Then I will take a vow to make another five million prostrations."

We shared tea together, and then I left to continue my walk through the foothills, leaving him to carry on with his commitment.

The Tibetan had found inner peace through his penance. Although his form of penance had apparently no direct relevance to the actions that had caused his remorse, his spiritual practice of prostrations enabled him to work through his deep regrets over his past violent actions. Many different religious traditions have acknowledged the deep inner significance of transformation through wise, honest, and sustained forms of penance to purify the heart. It is a spiritual practice that many of us could benefit from exploring further to heal our inner pain over our past actions. However, in the modern world, there is often little aptitude for such dedication. We prefer counseling or an instant solution to our wrongdoing and the harm that we have caused others or brought upon ourselves. Religious beliefs and practices may make all the difference to the quality of our lives, providing we bring to them the willingness to develop a commitment to change.

TRANSFORMING OUR FEARS

If we succumb to fear of any of the types outlined above, daily life becomes distressingly painful, and fear eats up any contentment and joy. Without realizing it, we can develop a deep sense of despair.

However, most of the time we pay little real attention to fear since it lies deep down in the psyche, where, unnoticed, it fuels our concerns, actions, and inaction. Because we are largely unaware of our underlying fears, we often find it hard to accept that these hold us back or influence our capacity to act, love, accept, or understand. If we do want to become more conscious, we need to stop and inquire within ourselves about whether fear dominates our responses. What shows fear? What shows fearlessness? What practical steps can be taken to make the transition from fear to fearlessness?

After a sudden loss or threat, fear quickly surfaces and penetrates our consciousness, producing varying degrees of emotional discomfort. We hate this entrapment in fear; we want to get out of it. Unable to cope with change in the present, we project the force of these fears into the future, which darkens our consciousness like a gathering storm. We unwittingly extend our fears until they become despair, or hysteria, or we keep replaying them in our minds as a disaster scenario with no end in sight. It takes powerful motivation from within and support from outside to break out of such a state of mind.

We have to develop the determination and courage to live with the way things are, even if this means never knowing from one day to the next whether what we fear will become reality. We need to work hard— personally, socially, and politically—to develop the capacity to transform fear, whether it is felt intensely in the moment or acts as an underlying influence upon decisions, as the following story illustrates.

A secretary had reached her 40th birthday when she started listening to an inner voice inside of her that kept telling her that she was wasting her life working five days a week in the city with her unused passport in the bottom drawer of her bedroom dresser. She had never felt particularly confident about herself, but she decided she had to do one brave thing in her life—quit her job and take a year to travel around the world. Quitting her job proved relatively easy, as did buying the tickets for her trip later in the year. After that, however, her fears started to increase. She said, "I seem to have a different fear about this trip for every day of the week." She knew she had to listen to her voice of courage rather than submit to her voice of fear. Three months later, she set off on the first part of her journey. Having conquered her fears, she was now able to open herself up to the enjoyment of her new freedom.

It would be foolish to imagine that there is a prescription available to overcome fear in whatever form it may arise. The Buddhist tradition encourages the application of what is described as the "opponent force"— namely courage. Reflections on change and death, the sense there is nothing to lose, inner empowerment, finding inspiration, and the support of others all serve as important resources once you have made up your mind to overcome the fear. You have to be clear about working to dissolve fear, and to be vigilant in keeping that determination in the forefront of consciousness daily. Then the rest will follow.

THE NATURE OF ANGER

After a traumatic event, when the waves of crying, sobbing, and grief have subsided, we may be left with a desire for revenge, a perceived need to inflict suffering upon those who have caused us such grief. As the gradual recovery from the initial shock takes place, the emotional, mental, and physical bodies begin to feel a renewal of energy. In spiritual terms, this is a critical time. What happens to that energy? How is it deployed? The risk is that the fresh energy will fasten on the negative thoughts that still linger, giving the mind the impetus to consider the harm it wants to inflict on those who have caused it harm. This is the origin of anger.

Some people manifest their anger by blasting their perceived enemy with blame, curses, personal abuse, and threats, finding it difficult, if not impossible, to take a detached view. Others find themselves affected in a quieter way; they do not shout or get into a state of uncontrollable fury, but nonetheless they still target somebody with their vengeful feelings, finding that the fault lies entirely with another.

It is terribly easy to justify anger and to rationalize its use as if there is no other way to deal with something that has upset us. On some major issues, we will even speak of "righteous" anger, claiming that such an anger fires us up to bring about social change. However, the determination to bring about change lasts as long as the anger is sustained. But whether anger is a sustainable force without becoming destructive needs examination. Anger is not in our control. It can turn upon anyone, including those who work for peace, justice, and reconciliation.

Self-righteous anger, whether expressed by a political leader in front of a crowd of supporters or an angry parent at home, says little about a situation and far more about the state of mind of the angry individual. There is no substitute for wisdom and compassion.

One of the main reasons for anger is to demonstrate or recover a sense of power. "They did this to me. They have to learn that they cannot treat me like this." It seems so clear. We believe that right and wrong, good and evil exist in watertight compartments. We see those who have provoked our righteous anger as wrong and perhaps even bad, so we have the right to make them suffer. Making the other—or others who have some connection with the main perpetrator of suffering—suffer gives us a sense of satisfaction in having regained power. The determination to get even serves as temporary relief, but the abused becomes the abuser. We need to remember that this projection of blame acts as a defense against having to look inward. In some cases, the injured party may have to admit a share of the responsibility.

We often look at events in terms of cause and effect in order to uphold our certainty in our interpretation of events. With this approach there is no possibility of exploring the variety of conditions that exist behind a simplistic cause–effect analysis. The mind is locked into a certain viewpoint, and we arrogantly dismiss any other way of examining what happened and why it happened. We are told that we are either on one side of a conflict or the other. The duality of the mind continues to be perpetuated.

When this stage is reached, the offender and the offended launch into a conflict where they have more in common than what divides them. Both are convinced that the first cause for the problem springs not from them but from the other. Nobody can persuade them to doubt their position. Blame acts as the justification for retaliation. Both sides use the past to rationalize their hatred of the other. Both want to see the other suffer.

Some people sustain their antagonism toward others not because it reflects truth in any way, but because they fear appearing naive. Naivete is probably the most common accusation to be thrown at those who advocate different responses to retaliation at whatever level. Yet maintaining an openness toward all points of view need not be a form of blind innocence, but a wise and considered means of moving out of the deadlock of confrontation.

Those who pursue retaliation may find themselves unable to reach the original offender. Instead, this negative force, marshaled in our consciousness, has to find another focus. It turns on the self, on to loved ones, or those associated, however remotely, with those who caused us harm. This process is exemplified in the following story.

Three young women went on their first holiday together to a tourist center in southern Turkey, where they had rented an apartment on the ground floor of a holiday complex. From the first day, nothing went right. For much of each day a gang of local youths hung around the front of their apartment shouting and yelling at them to come out. They threw stones at their door. The women's clothes were stolen from their washing line. They found themselves afraid to go out. The management of the apartment complex, although sympathetic, said they could do nothing.

Having spent months saving and planning for their trip, the three tourists spent the days talking about their plight and the daily harassment they were experiencing. At times, they were in tears. They could not wait for their holiday to finish and to get back home.

Two of the women left the country with a painful impression of their visit. From that time on, they spoke only of their contempt for the country and its people. Out of their experience of a particular situation, they formed crude generalizations. However, the third woman put aside her anger and fear and went back to Turkey for a successful holiday the following year.

We often wonder how some people are able to stay free from the shadow of the past. Unlike her two friends, the woman who returned to Turkey had enough awareness and clarity to realize that a single painful incident did not define a whole country. It is this awareness that makes the difference between those who remain stuck in the past and those who can move on. As a spiritual practice, awareness is the key to change. We do not always have to ask "how" in terms of inner change. Instead, we bring the fullness of awareness to a situation and respond wholeheartedly to it so that the present perception matters more than the past.

The processes that lead to anger can occur at all levels of human interaction: between nations, communities, and between individuals. Much conflict goes on in the home, as was experienced by the following couple, who had been married for several years. The wife had started to have doubts about how much longer she could tolerate her husband's anger toward her. Acting like a dark force over their relationship, he constantly threw abuse at her on the slightest pretext. He made her life unbearable. She spent much of her time watching television, talking on the telephone to her friends, spending money on clothes, and rarely initiated a conversation with him. He felt that he needed to get really angry to gain her attention. He seemed convinced that if she responded more quickly to his needs then he would have no reason to work himself up into a rage. It was only when he started yelling at her that he realized how much the shadow of his intolerance and her indifference to him hung over their marriage. For change to take place, he had to develop a mindfulness of his intolerance and the willingness to change. She had to learn to give him the attention he needed. It took genuine cooperation from both partners to extricate themselves from the loop. Each had to acknowledge their own role in their marriage problems.

Although this is a domestic example, it is easy to find parallels between such situations and international strife. Governments have to learn to listen to rather than attack each other. Indifference and resentment often pass from one generation to another, with differences becoming inflamed at times. It is easy to forget that at times of national crisis our leaders often behave like a fractious married couple, with each trying to make the life of the other as miserable as possible. Our attitude says more about ourselves than we perceive. Blame and retaliation or using charged words like "hateful" or "evil" block our capacity and freedom of mind to examine with insight our relationship with others. Absolute positions of right and wrong rarely tell us much about the totality of a situation.

The Buddha said: "Anger does not cease with anger. Anger ceases through non-anger." We do not have to love those whom we perceive, rightly or wrongly, as a threat, but we can work toward understanding them as part of the healing process. If we allow ourselves to be caught up in a negative and cynical attitude, we may blindly assume that our distorted views reflect reality. We must remember that relationships can change only when authentic listening and compassionate actions take place.

The capacity to maintain awareness of negative attitudes safeguards us from falling into the trap of anger and retaliation. This demanding reflection, this act of soul-searching, expresses a capacity to look at a situation as a whole rather than from a one-sided viewpoint. A crude perception of the differences gives license for revenge. We then use brute force to gain the upper hand, which demonizes others until they become utterly associated with a negative perception, as though it is the ultimate truth of the matter. Deep reflection and wise responses to events show a mature and civilized approach.

We need to continue believing in the deep qualities of human existence, to remain true to them through thick and thin, rather than ignore them. Otherwise, we fall back on reactive tendencies and arrogant ways of dealing with those who do not agree with us or may even dislike us. People's lives become blighted through harboring resentment, whether it is between a child and his or her parents, a colleague at work, an employer and employee, or the other side in an international conflict. We are not only a problem for others through our attitude but we are an enemy to ourselves, since it undermines peace and contentment within. Instead of feeling angry toward people who are hostile and cynical, we need to feel compassion, since their state of mind blocks off natural happiness. The role of deeply spiritual people is to find the resolve to help dissolve the driving forces of fear and anger, conscious or unconscious, in daily life so that two new "weapons" for change make their impact—namely insight and compassion.

In August 1941, Etty Hillesum, a 27-year-old Jewish woman, waited in her apartment in Amsterdam, the Netherlands, not knowing from one day to the next when she would be deported to a concentration camp. She wrote in her diary "I can't really voice what is really going on inside of me. There is nothing else for it. I shall have to solve my own problems. I always get the feeling that when I solve them for myself I shall have solved them for a thousand other women. For that very reason, I must come to grips with myself. Sometimes I long for a convent cell with the sublime wisdom of centuries. There must be cornfields and they must wave in the breeze. Then perhaps I might find peace and clarity. But that would be no great feat. It is right here, in this very place, in the here and now, that I must find them."

MEDITATION ON NAMING THE SUFFERING

Use this meditation to help clarify your thoughts, particularly at times of emotional stress when fear and anger can easily take hold.

• Here and now, I recognize that this problem is arising.

• I am aware of the impact it has due to its arising.

• I am aware of the feelings, thoughts, and intentions that form this state of mind.

• I am aware of how easily its momentum comes out through what I say and do.

• I am aware of the degree to which I identify with this state of mind and justify it.

• It not only makes life difficult for myself but also makes life difficult for others.

• Here and now I have the opportunity to work with this state of mind.

• Here and now I am practicing to let go of this state of mind.

• Here and now I am practicing to stop grasping onto this situation.

• I am aware that this state of mind only comes from a similar state of mind in the past.

• Right now, I have the opportunity to develop freedom from this state of mind.

• Right now, I have the opportunity to see the emptiness of this state of mind.

• This opportunity is available to me here and now.

There are six questions worth asking ourselves as we attend to episodes of fear and anger in our lives. We could write out each of the questions, then write our responses out honestly. Then follow up on the action that shows wisdom and understanding. The first two questions refer to the past. The second two questions refer to the present. The last two questions refer to the future.

1. What have I done?
2. What have I not done?
3. What I am doing?
4. What am I not doing?
5. What have I got to do?
6. What have I not got to do?

CHAPTER FOUR

Coming to Terms with Death

For to the one that is born death is certain

Therefore for what is unavoidable, thou should not grieve.

To action alone you have a right,

Let not the fruits of action be your motive;

Neither let there be any attachment to inaction.

Krishna
Bhagavad Gita 27, 47

AS THE QUOTATION at the start of this chapter states,

death is a certainty in life. Yet despite knowing this to be so, most of us find it is the hardest thing to come to terms with. Fear of our own death and of losing those we love can become overwhelming. Yet it is possible for some people, when death approaches and is clearly unavoidable, to develop an unexpected calmness and clarity.

This was poignantly illustrated by some of the harrowing calls made from mobile phones in the hijacked aircraft and from within the doomed World Trade Center on September 11. Knowing their death was close, several passengers and employees sent messages of love to their relatives without dwelling on their own fears. One caller focused on his faith, reciting the Lord's Prayer with a telephone operator.

Many of us have known or heard of people who have faced death in less dramatic circumstances with equanimity and serenity, expressing concern for others above themselves. To achieve this sort of attitude it is important that we reflect upon how we feel about the prospect of our own mortality, the loss of loved ones, and the issue of suicide.

DENYING DEATH

On the whole, Western society treats old age and the unremitting wearing out of the body and its functions with a certain distaste. We do not easily accept the fact that we grow old and infirm. The demands of our consumer-led culture mean that most of us have made our work and the sustaining of self-interest our main priorities. So we find the infirmity of age a time-consuming liability, and attending to the needs of the sick and elderly can often seem an intrusion into lifestyles based on pleasure and satisfaction.

With the pursuit of pleasure seemingly held up by our society as the supreme purpose of existence, it is hardly surprising that aging, dying, and death tend to be hidden from public view and that we try to avoid looking at anything that will upset us in any way. The effort to maximize pleasure

MEDITATION ON THE BODY

Living in a culture obsessed with beautiful bodies, sex, clothes, cosmetics, and appearance, we rarely, if at all, meditate on the body as coming from nature, belonging to nature, and returning to nature. We have placed the demands of the self upon the body instead of respecting and supporting it. Meditating on the body is always useful. By doing it we can see the body as an instrument for service through which we can find a balanced relationship with our physical presence and a deep acceptance of change and death. Follow these steps:

1. Sit in a chair with a straight back, chin slightly tucked in. Place your feet firmly on the ground, a few inches apart. Your eyes are closed, and both hands rest in your lap, one hand resting in the palm of the other with the ends of both thumbs touching.

2. Turn your attention to the body. Move your attention down through the body from the top of the head through to the ends of the toes. Experience as much as possible from within. Feel the vibrations, throbbing, and tingling in the body as the power of attention passes moment to moment through it.

3. Then repeat the meditation exercise beginning with the toes and moving up through the body to the top of the head. Take several minutes to travel in each direction. Keep the posture upright, with shoulders back and chest and diaphragm open.

4. If your mind wanders, try to come back to the place in the body where it started to wander.

5. Experience the body as individual elements, as organic life, as expressions of nature.

6. Simply receive experiences of the body as they unfold. Treat all experiences as coming from nature and belonging to nature, rather than being self-made, self-created.

7. Let go of clinging to the body, possessiveness around the body, and self-image around the body.

8. Embrace the presence and absence of physical life without fear or attachment.

can perhaps be seen as an escape from the necessity to contemplate the final cessation of it—the fading away of the senses and the loss of consciousness linked to the senses.

We prefer to keep ourselves busy rather than take real time out to reflect on life and death. We hardly dare admit to ourselves that from one perspective a human life consists of nothing more than a blip in universal existence. If we did, all our worries about petty, trivial matters that beset our daily existence would cease.

There is nowhere we can hide from impending death. Its prospect can generate a terror like no other because it ensures that we are finally separated from all that is known and familiar, loved, or hated. We invest things with a fetishist significance. Although it is hard to accept, much of what we do is futile. And because we lack the inner resources to reflect on death, we cling to life, to the sense of self and what we have gathered in the course of time.

Some proclaim with a certain amount of confidence that they have no fear of death, of leaving this world. Such words mean little when uttered by those who are healthy or live in the midst of relative comfort and security because they believe that death is a distant, unreal prospect. There are also those who display a genuine fearlessness that has emerged naturally or through training. Soldiers, for example, are willing to die to fulfill the orders of their superiors. Yet these same soldiers often find that their unexamined fears burst into consciousness in other ways—perhaps in their fear of rejection, separation, disability, humiliation, or cowardice. Fear is only one emotion, but it finds many outlets for its expression; and the examination of fear enables us to get to the roots of insecurity, whether personal, social, or international.

If we inquire deeply into these feelings of insecurity around dying and death, we may awaken to another dimension that is free from sorrow and change and from which the world of birth, life, and death seems like a phantom reality. This inquiry into the ultimate security offers the greatest challenge for human beings.

REFLECTING ON DEATH

Of all the many religious traditions, Buddhism has perhaps examined our relationship to death the best. Buddhists are strongly encouraged to reflect on death, even though it may produce a morbid response in those who are prone to anxiety. Reflection on death also has the power to bring life into sharp focus: a clear awareness of the power of the here and now can act as an open doorway to a realization of the transcendent.

In the Buddhist monasteries of insight meditation, or Vipassana practice, it is not unusual to find corpses of monks hanging in glass boxes, skulls with photographs of what their owners looked like when alive placed beside them, and graphic paintings of an individual going through the aging process from birth to 100 years, showing the rise and decrepit fall of the body. Corpses are brought into the monastery for cremation with their faces clearly visible. These reminders are used, along with meditation and reflection, to break down the resistance to death and the fear that goes with it.

Monks and nuns go to morgues to see those who have died only minutes before. There are meditations and practices on death, impermanence, and letting go that point to the true, steadfast reality in the here and now. This reality neither comes nor goes, nor undergoes change. We, however, find ourselves caught up in the world of changing appearances, of birth, living, dying, and death.

Some people think that the practice of reflecting on death is morbid. The sight of a corpse often brings a grimace to the faces of those who enter Vipassana monasteries for the first time. And visitors to some Christian monasteries can see thousands of skulls of dead monks that are kept in the basement of the building to remind those living in the rooms above that death is never far away. Yet these relics have a positive purpose as visible reminders of our impermanence. They can help us to become deeply at ease with existence and nonexistence and to realize that ultimately the things of this world fall into neither of these categories.

In spiritual life, one of the most difficult teachings to comprehend is this realization of nonduality, which embraces such categories as existence and nonexistence. In everyday life, we seem to experience a whole range of dualities:

- birth and death
- health and sickness
- coming and going
- presence and absence
- good and evil
- gain and loss
- success and failure
- praise and blame
- here and there
- us and them
- you and me.

We have become so involved in dualities that we honestly believe that clinging to one side of a duality and resisting the other side constitutes what life is all about. Through spiritual practice, however, we come to see the emptiness of duality and discover nonduality through interconnection, understanding, and expansive freedom.

FACING UP TO DEATH

As we get older, it often seems that each year passes by quicker than the year before. We find ourselves talking more and more about health issues, about people we know who are sick, dying, or have passed away. These are central issues of life from which we cannot protect ourselves through prosperity, possessions, and position. In the face of the reality that we are all destined to die and cannot predict when and from what our lives will end, we question the values of secular culture and look to explore different perspectives on our time on earth. True religion can point us in the right direction, although we need to be mindful of not becoming ensnared in dogmatic religious beliefs.

What is most important of all is gaining a deep and abiding sense of something spiritual in daily life that transcends the demands and expectations of our ego. If we meditate on death regularly, with honesty and understanding, then the power of our meditations will place us firmly in touch with the spiritual mystery of life and the great web of existence.

At first we may react negatively to meditating on death. If the meditation undermines our sense of purpose and prompts us to ask ourselves "What's the point of doing anything? We are all going to die anyway," we must try to see this as an initial reaction. In time, meditation on death opens the heart to the expanse of life. It can reveal that:

• Life is precious and vulnerable.

• What human beings have in common is greater than what separates them.

• Our awareness of death brings humility into our lives.

• We can make life an adventure.

If death is to lose its significance through meditation and renouncing the desire for the things in life that make us resist death, then the supposed reality of time must also fade so that we can grasp the presence of what exists beyond it. Through observation and meditation, our unconventional experiences, insights, and understanding can enter into our consciousness. There is a simple key to bring about this transformation of perceptions. That key is the total attention to the here and now, no matter what is happening. Death has no hold for those whose consciousness has burst the bubble of conventional existence, with all its fears and flaws that act like a tyranny upon a free and immeasurable way of living.

COPING WITH DEATH

For most people, coping with the death of a loved one is extraordinarily difficult. The differences between life and death seem absolute. In bereavement, psychologists have recognized what they refer to as a "grief process." Many pass through the following sequence of emotional events as they adjust to the loss of an important person in their lives. The stages are not necessarily experienced in a particular order, however. Some people may move backward and forward in varying degrees among them. Others experience a definite movement from one stage to another, a transition that may take days, weeks, or much longer.

There are generally four stages in this grief process:

1 | A SENSE OF NUMBNESS

This feeling is often associated with disbelief. The bereaved refuse to accept the reality of the death, and they may lack the ability to release waves of emotion into consciousness. Their inner lives feel empty, and they seem to lose their sense of association with the world. They tend to be very quiet, often only repeating words like "It can't be true. It can't be true. Please say it is not true."

MEDITATING ON DEATH

Perhaps you have lost a loved one, or know someone close to you who is grieving, who will find this meditation helpful. Read the words quietly, or take up your usual meditation posture. Try to absorb the feelings that these words evoke. This may be difficult at first because death is, for most of us, a threatening prospect. Practice will remove initial fears and instill a sense of calm.

• One day ... I will no longer wake up in the morning. I will no longer have access to the everyday. There will no longer be any contact with those I love.

• I do not know if I will die slowly or quickly. I do not know what percentage of my life is over. I might die today or tomorrow or years from now.

• This whole journey through life will slide to a halt. There will be no more vanity to my brief visit to this earth.

• I cannot put my life back to birth and start again. I cannot move it forward and see myself further down the road.

• This unfolding existence carries me along in the grace of the unknown, where one global catastrophe can destroy 10,000 years of human development.

• Can I dissolve the barriers dividing life from death? What am I going to do with the rest of my wild, uncertain, breathtaking existence?

News of a loss can leave a person in a deep state of shock, as was the case in the following tragic story. A young man was on a business trip and had promised to telephone his parents upon his arrival. The parents waited all day for their son to telephone. Very late that evening, the telephone finally rang. The parents rushed to answer, thinking it was their son calling to say he was safe. It was an airline representative expressing his regret. The plane had crashed. Their son had died. The bereaved often experience a sense of the unreality of everything as the emotions lock into the self as a kind of protection from experiencing the full impact of the loss. For days the parents expected their son to walk through the front door with his usual "Hi, Mom, hi, Dad" greeting.

It is hard to communicate in words the depth of shock and numbness that impacts upon the emotional life. Physically, it is like falling out of a tree, having all the air knocked out of your body and feeling a pervasive numbness. The heart is devastated, the mind cannot think straight and there is a sense of great pain. For some, the shock is so penetrating that it is not even possible to cry. Sudden bereavement is one of the hardest experiences a human being has to face. Those who suffer it must remain quietly determined to get through this difficult period.

2 | YEARNING FOR A LOVED ONE

Once there is recognition of the loss, then there is a yearning for contact with the deceased. This may express itself through staying close to their possessions, calling out their name, talking to them, or imagining them in heaven. The bereaved keep remembering happy incidents from the past and search for evidence—letters, photographs, and so on—to show that the deceased still has a significant presence in the world. This period of time may release many emotions, ranging from sorrow to anger, as the bereaved endeavor to adjust to a major change in their lives as well as an overwhelming sense of loss.

For some, the death of a deeply loved person does not dissolve the relationship but instead enhances it: the living person feels that the deceased is actually in the immediate vicinity. In cases of long-standing marriages or relationships, those who live may consult with the dead before making important decisions. The responses they receive may differ from what they expect.

Such cases show that the great divide between life and death may be less substantial than we commonly think. A couple had been married for more than 50 years, rarely spending a day apart. Then the husband's health began to deteriorate and after a few weeks he quietly passed away. After the funeral and cremation, his widow returned home to try to adjust to living alone. To her surprise, she felt she was not alone; she could sense the quiet presence of her husband in some inexplicable way. She felt the experiences of bereavement were not as black and white as she had believed.

3 | A PERIOD OF UNCERTAINTY

As the bereaved come to terms with the loss of a loved one, they often feel life has no direction and meaning. They do not know how to continue any longer without the presence of the loved one. They have little or no appetite to find any regular rhythm or order in their lives. In this stage of transition, despair may arise due to the lack of any passion to do anything. Uncertainty about the future may become manifest through streams of thoughts running through the mind, or the lack of them.

Conversations tend to be in the negative rather than purposeful, as the inner voice struggles to find a new path while remaining respectful to the memory of the deceased. One reason it is hard to adapt to bereavement is the fact that some people have to steer their lives in a new direction. Then anguish about the future and past events fuse together.

At such times, the practice of taking one day at a time really matters. The inner life, especially the emotions, need to recover their vitality and energy. There is no point in living in the past, nor blindly rushing into something new that we may regret later, as the following story illustrates. It was a couple's tenth wedding anniversary. She secretly organized a party for their family and friends for him at home to start when he arrived home from work. It was just before Christmas. On the way home, he was knocked down and killed by a drunk driver. Instead of her husband knocking on the front door, it was two police officers bringing her the tragic news.

She came to realize that she needed a period of calm and stability, even though initially she wanted to get away from her home. She used the following weeks to take stock of her life, and spend more time with her friends and family, rather than rush into making decisions born from sorrow and panic.

4 | A NEW MODE OF LIFE

This stage reveals that the bereaved has entered the period of recovery, although painful experiences associated with the first, second, or third stage may still arise. The inner life force begins to reassert itself. The bereaved feel a renewed capacity to reorganize their lives knowing that life moves on. They can remember the deceased without floods of tears or feelings of despair, and they develop a growing sense of accepting the loss. Grief is temporary and dissolves. Clinging to the past and refusing to come to terms with change inhibits access to this final stage in the process of grief, or at least slows it down.

Finally, there comes an awareness that the closing of one door opens a new door of opportunity or at least of understanding. Aged in their mid-30s, a couple worked together teaching in higher education. They had been partners since the age of 20. He complained of stomach pains and within six weeks died from stomach cancer. She told me "My life changed in every way. The love of my life died. Income was cut exactly in half. I had to move to a cheaper apartment and live on a lot less money. After I had gone through this very painful loss, I saw fresh opportunities for my life. Light began to transform this dark period."

DEATH AND BEYOND

With regard to what happens to us after death there seem to be four possible beliefs to place our trust in. We might hold that:

1. Death brings total extinction. We live once. We die once. That is it. This view is the prevalent one in what might be called the religion of Scientific Materialism.

2. Death brings rebirth or reincarnation. We are like waves in the ocean of life, rising and falling according to the forces that bring us into the world and take us out of it.

3. At death we become disembodied spirits or abide in a very fine material realm, far more refined than the gross physical realm we are familiar with.

4. After death, we go to an eternal heaven or hell according to our particular religious beliefs and actions in this world.

It is not easy to fathom why we lean more toward one view more than another. Are we influenced by secular society? Do religion and culture influence us? Have we thought it through? Have we had personal experiences that have shaped our views about death and the afterlife? There is no absolute knowledge about whether there is life after death or no life after death. At best, we can only have an open mind.

Some people rely totally on sense perceptions for their view of life, death, and extinction, while others believe that the non-material force of life moves on into new forms. The prospect of reincarnation can hold out consolation or induce anxiety, depending on the individual's moral actions in his or her current life.

Those who believe they will enter the kingdom of God after death probably perceive a difference between life on Earth and life in Heaven. If their lot on Earth is wretched, heaven offers them hope. Yet if we are able to see deeply into the here and now, then it is possible to realize that "the Kingdom of God is at hand," thus dissolving perceived differences between life and death.

For those who are truly liberated, questions about death and the afterlife have ceased to be an issue, since they know that to abide in true reality is to abide in a realm that knows no death.

Some people, it seems, have supernatural experiences involving sensory contact with the departed. For them—as with those who feel the presence of a dead loved one in a nonsupernatural way—the difference between life and death appears to be blurred. One woman reported that for months after her husband passed away, she felt the weight of his presence in bed beside her. Another said she could hear the voice of her husband giving her advice to cope with daily matters. One son said his mother told him after she died that he had nothing to worry about as far as death was concerned. Some psychiatrists claim that such experiences are merely hallucinations. Others think they confirm the possibility of communication from the dead to the living—or vice versa. Fearing ridicule, people are often reluctant to confide in others about such experiences, which actually neither confirm nor deny an otherworldly reality but show the kind of changes that take place when bereavement affects a person's perceptions. Some view apparent contact with the deceased as a form of unconscious denial that they have died. What is noticeable is that these experiences of reconnection can continue long after the actual death and that the living person may show no sign whatsoever of emotional disturbance, hallucinatory tendencies, or unhealthy expressions of mental behavior.

Finally, it is equally important to recognize that some people are not concerned with any notion of an afterlife and regard death as the completion of a relationship. The loved one lived and the loved one died. End of story. This sense of completion allows the bereaved to move on with their lives. They feel gratitude for the period of time they spent with their loved ones without cherishing any thoughts that they live on in some way or other; nor do they have any hope of a future reunion after death. We can keep faith only with our own particular experience.

SUICIDE AND ITS AFTERMATH

A decision to take your own life happens when the force of desire within opts for nonexistence over existence, or nonbeing over being. Although some are driven along that route for a variety of reasons and causes, we feel deep down that it is not the answer to dealing with the problems of existence, whether personal or collective. There are exceptional circumstances, however, when sustaining life for its own sake causes us to question the general principle of protection of life.

THE CAUSES OF SUICIDE

Alcohol, drug abuse, and mental illness often form the primary conditions for many suicides. For some people, from students to senior citizens, there is simply a personal anguish, a bleak hopelessness that intensifies and precipitates a desire to end their lives. Those who are severely depressed or distraught may find it hard to express themselves in a way that makes them feel they have been heard and understood. When people feel deeply tormented they are especially vulnerable.

COPING WITH SUICIDE

People often report that those they know who committed suicide seem to have undergone a change in personality once they planned the time and date of their death. This is because before making the decision to end their lives, people often express despair, confusion, and various suicidal thoughts. Then they secretly make the decision to end their lives and, having done so, feel a degree of calmness through having a focus. They relax and exercise control over their feelings. Their responses to others give no indication of their carefully laid plans to kill themselves. Those who have planned suicide have moved beyond the inner torment of whether to live or to die.

This was the case for one man who had become depressed after losing his job. Under severe financial pressure, he felt that there was no point in continuing his life. He had a wife and child, whose lives he made hard to bear as he withdrew from any kind of loving contact with them into a mood of lifeless despair. Then he changed, becoming relaxed, quiet, and more communicative. He no longer referred to his anxieties about paying the mortgage or losing their home.

One afternoon, his wife went to pick up their child from school. As she opened the front door of the apartment, she saw her husband hanging from a rope with his feet dangling beside the chair. She quickly covered her son's eyes. Gas was pouring out of the kitchen, where her husband had turned all the gas jets on the stove on high.

The following day she told her best friend through her tears: "I don't understand why he would kill himself over his inability to pay monthly bills. He knew I didn't care if we had to leave the place and move into rented quarters. Most of all I can't understand why he turned the gas jets on. Did he want to kill my son and me and blow up the whole building?"

It was vital at such a time of confusion and despair that the wife felt the support and presence of loving family and friends to enable her to move through this time of great anguish as quickly as possible. Otherwise she faced the risk of constant self-recrimination when she remembered their arguments over money or things that she said and now regretted. As with so many of these distressing events in human existence, there is no quick fix, no prescription for rapid self-healing. We can only make use of inner and outer resources. We need to take one day at a time, keep focused as much as possible on present activities, talk with loved ones, spend time outdoors, and generate loving kindness to the one who died in such a confused state of mind.

SUICIDE AND KILLING

Those who attempt suicide may wish to seek the attention of others, who they feel have hurt them in some way or other. Such desperate needs deserve to be responded to with all the love and compassion we can muster. Others seek to draw attention to a cause, so they become willing to die in a suicide attack on others whom they blame for the situation they wish to change.

In the early 1990s, I met briefly with the late prime minister of Sri Lanka when he was on a state visit to Bodh Gaya, India, the village where the Buddha was enlightened some 2,500 years ago. Three months later, a young woman with explosives strapped to her chest approached the prime minister and several of his staff at a public outdoor function in Colombo, the capital of Sri Lanka. She triggered the device, killing a dozen people, including the prime minister himself. His body was recognizable only by a ring on his finger.

Clearly, this kind of murderous suicide falls into a category that differs from that of the suicide born from personal despair. The idea to kill both herself and a major political figure simultaneously must have taken a deeply rooted hold in the woman's psyche to the exclusion of all else. Presumably fueled by painful memories and political and religious beliefs, and manipulated by others professing the same beliefs, she embarked on a course of action to kill and die in the process. It did nothing to resolve the plight of her community in Sri Lanka, and perhaps only invited more suffering for those whose lives she believed she was acting on behalf of.

There is a pathology behind those who take such drastic, suicidal steps to support what they believe to be the greater good. Such individuals do not consider their deaths to be suicide. They regard their actions as the price for making war on those they see have caused their community so much suffering. Individuals who blow themselves up on a crowded street regard the loss of their life as a small price to pay.

Soldiers go into battle prepared to kill others and die for the cause they believe in. When one soldier first shot and killed another person in Kosovo, he felt sick to the stomach. He thought about the suffering he had caused the young man's family and friends. He wanted to throw his rifle away, hating himself and war itself. That night, he reported he could not sleep because he was so racked with guilt. His commanding officer told him he would get used to it.

The next day, the young soldier found himself at the front line again, this time killing another two men and wounding more. Again, he felt sick and disgusted with himself and with the primitive savagery of it all. Within a few days, he had become used to killing and seeing death all around him. He got back into the habit of sleeping well at night. Within a few weeks, he told other young soldiers, who felt equally sick at killing other human beings, that they would get used to it within a couple of weeks. Yet, such experiences often leave soldiers traumatized when they return home. The emotional and psychological cost for time on the battlefield is high—sometimes resulting in depression and suicide.

It is extraordinarily difficult to transform the hurt and the pain caused to people through the intentions of organizations to kill others deliberately or the military exercising a shoot-to-kill policy for their cause. Such suffering, suicides, and killings reveal hell on Earth. It is the task of spiritual awareness to find constructive engagement rather than destructive engagement for the welfare of all in the short and long term. All those who face suffering, suicide, and death deserve our love, concern, and compassion.

MEDITATION ON THE UNKNOWN

There are times in our lives when we have to face the unknown. It may be with regard to the future, when we have no idea how events will turn out and so find ourselves thinking about all the possibilities. The purpose of this meditation is to learn to stay true to the fact that we have to live without knowledge of outcomes. There may be specific situations of stress, as when prisoners are waiting for the outcome of a trial or an appeal, or patients are wondering about the results of their tests. At such moments, meditating on the unknown may help to achieve peace of mind. There are also times when we realize how little we know about anything. The unknown conveys wonder, mystery, and the sense of innocence and humility in life. Such a meditation keeps us in touch with the depths of mystery that pervade all of this existence. If you find you are fearful of anything, take up your usual meditation posture and think about the following, slowly and mindfully.

1. Contemplate the fact that we know little of this world, and that what we do know comes through our senses, memory, and intuitive and instinctive responses.
2. Consider that we do not know the time when major events will happen and know little of what life has in store for us.
3. Reflect on the fact that events unfold through our lives, some of them anticipated, some of them coming to us utterly unexpectedly.
4. Affirm the following thoughts with confidence:

• Let us find the strength and determination to take steps into the unknown, to step outside our familiar constructions in personal, social, and national life.

• Let us learn to experience the unknown as a challenge rather than a threat, as an opportunity for clarity and wisdom rather than the destruction of it.

• Let us not fill the unknown with lots of speculative thoughts, but embrace it so that it fills our consciousness, giving our life mystery and immeasurable opportunity.

• Let us allow beginnings and endings, life and death, to rest in the mystery of the unknown so that we stay fully in tune with this unfathomable existence.

CHAPTER FIVE

Looking into Stereotypes

There is no greater illusion than fear

No greater wrong than preparing to defend yourself

No greater misfortune than having an enemy,

Whoever can see through all fear will always be safe.

Nothing is impossible for him

Because he has let go,

He can care for the people's welfare.

Lao Tzu
Tao Te Ching 46, 59

 ON MY WALL at home I have had hanging for several years a color photograph of myself standing next to two young men in Afghanistan in the heart of the barren, somewhat uninviting desert that stretches between Kandahar and Kabul. The picture was taken in my early 20s when I was traveling overland to India via the Muslim nations of Turkey, Iran, Afghanistan, and Pakistan. I was able to see firsthand the harsh environment of rocks, sand, and scattered villages and haphazardly built towns, in which the impoverished people of Afghanistan have had to endure violent internal conflicts as well as the wrath of powerful Western nations.

I often wonder what happened to those two young men, taking care of their beloved camels in the desert? Have they survived the bullets and bombs of this present conflict? I can still recall the endless expressions of kind hospitality that I received from people in these Muslim nations. Hardly a soul spoke English, so we exchanged information through gestures, good humor, acts of kindness, and hospitality. I was given rides in battered cars, lumbering trucks, and run-down windowless buses packed tight with local people on their way to the market in nearby towns.

A young Englishman, traveling with a small backpack containing a worn-out sleeping bag, a change of clothes, a couple of books, very little money, and a camera, clearly posed no threat to anyone. As such, I benefited from these rugged and proud peoples' hospitality, which is a central tenet of the Islamic faith. That overland journey, which took me to more than 30 countries, helped form my thinking and my education. Travel can broaden the mind, and those who harbor prejudices against another country usually do so out of ignorance; and it is ignorance that inspires fear.

Also, I believe I learned to distinguish between ordinary people and governments, between civilians and military forces. Yet here, too, we can fall into the trap of fixing stereotypes. Every politician, soldier, and religious leader moves in and out of that role. The same person may also be a parent, father, brother, son, husband, wife, mother, daughter, or close friend. No role stands in isolation from other ones.

We tend to overlook these simple truths when, in acts of violence or war, we launch the forces of negativity upon others, blinding ourselves as we cast our dark shadows onto the stage of human history. For an inviolable spiritual ethic to govern our vision, we must look deeply into ourselves, our own culture, beliefs, and society. We must forget our hardened views and make time to understand how others see us. Such inner and outer reflection will help protect the precious and vulnerable nature of life and especially the right of men, women, and children to feel understood.

Stereotypes and prejudices have their roots in the human psyche and are bred from fear and ignorance. These are the two main factors that create the sort of blinkered and intolerant thinking that can lead to aggression and physical violence. Most of us need to realize that the spiritual response to the problem of stereotypes is to bring our suppressed or ill-recognized feelings of insecurity and antagonism to the surface of consciousness so they can be properly dealt with. As the quotation from the *Tao Te Ching* at the beginning of the chapter states, "Whoever can see through all fear will always be safe."

THE PROBLEM OF STEREOTYPES

Stereotyping is the practice of making generalizations about people and things. But the danger with this is that we tend to reduce complexity and variety to crude images or caricatures. It is not surprising, therefore, that most of us resist being regarded as stereotypes since we feel they lump us into a category with others and portray us in a way that is both simplistic and difficult to alter.

Likewise, thoughtful people resist using stereotypes since they can appreciate that others will find their use offensive. Yet despite this reluctance to make hackneyed, generalizing comments, we still repeat them in both positive and negative ways whenever we speak of a country or group of people in collective terms, for example, "the French are wonderful cooks" or "the English are xenophobic" or "the Canadians are conventional" and so on.

Stereotypes like these may serve to give a quick sketch of common traits in groups of people. But the problem is that through these images we tend to focus on negative traits and deny the positive ones, or vice versa. We then generate prejudiced information about our experiences of nations, political or religious beliefs, or groups of people, reducing them to clichéd pictures that we hold onto as unchangeable truths. These pictures can then start to matter more than the human beings behind them and lead to a black-and-white view of human nature.

Furthermore, negative stereotypes can easily intensify in the mind and lead to impatience with, and intolerance of, others. This process, at its most extreme, can spur a country or a group to make war, commit acts of violence, and engage in suicide attacks.

It is important to look at the typical psychological and emotional development of those intent on violence, whose attitude is marked by an unquestioning loyalty to stereotyped pictures that are divorced from real people and real lives. This happens unconsciously rather than consciously. The problem starts when our negative feelings increasingly consolidate around a word that defines a group of people. In the current climate, the charged word might be "Americans" or "Muslims." Rather than unpack the diverse meanings, associations, and nuances in the word, we project onto it a range of views that build up with greater and greater intensity over time. Failing to question this pattern, we feed the stereotyped image until it becomes embedded in the psyche. Once it is firmly fixed there, we experience a corresponding resistance to examining it. Instead, we become utterly and irrevocably convinced of the absolute rightness of our position and our moral authority.

The conflict started by the events of September 11, 2001, acts as a metaphor for all other conflicts, past, present, and future. Typically, two sides, persuaded of their own position, share a similar antagonistic attitude toward each other and emphasize the differences between them, even though they may have more in common than they care to admit. The process of stereotyping "the enemy" affects not only perceptions but also judgments, which in turn inform the actions that affect countless numbers of innocent people. For example, in the present conflict, Western tourists have canceled their holidays to countries with significant numbers of Muslims for fear of being stereotyped as backers of their governments' foreign policy; male passengers have been ordered off an aircraft from Sweden to Spain because they looked Middle Eastern; and damage has been inflicted on mosques in the West and churches in Pakistan.

In such a climate of conflict and mutual stereotyping, we think that our lives matter far more than the lives of others in other parts of the world. We lack the capacity to shed tears for all the innocent people who die horrendous deaths elsewhere. It is relatively easy to spot the failings of others seemingly far removed from our own culture; it is much harder to look at ourselves.

So we have a responsibility to look at the way we absorb and create stereotypical images and their painful consequences. For if we can become aware of the stereotypes we hold and how they form inside us, we can begin to understand their effect on us and so deal with them. In recent years, sociologists have done significant research into these destructive images, which have become the breeding ground for hatred and are used to promulgate intolerance of others through crude literature, public speeches, certain web sites, or videos.

Some forms of media naturally lend themselves to stereotyping. Newspapers, for example, often resort to stereotype clichés. And movies, which aim to make an instant impact, often shrink complex characters and situations to types, such as "good guys" and "bad guys."

It is easy to spot instances of stereotyping in the media. But we are all responsible for perpetuating it in our portrayals of people from a particular country, culture, or of a particular religion, color, age, gender, or sexual orientation. Most of us are hardly aware of the frequency with which we resort to stereotyped pictures of people in a way that is far more eloquent about our attitudes than we may perceive, as these two examples illustrate.

A young female student arrived in London from Iran. At the airport, she bought a coach ticket and then afterward realized she had a student card that would give her a discount. She asked the woman issuing her ticket to change it to a cheaper one. The woman got very irritated. After replacing the ticket, she turned to her colleague and remarked: "These people from the Middle East should go back to where they came from."

A young Western female student went to Pakistan to study the religion and culture. She said she found herself being treated with disrespect. In the hot weather, she wore short sleeves and long, cotton pants and this attire, although unremarkable by Western standards, made various young men treat her as if she were sexually available. She felt stereotyped as a particular kind of person.

We need awareness to catch our tendency toward using generalizations that describe individuals in terms of the groups they represent. To overcome this habit and to reveal our use of stereotyping, it may be helpful to consider the following points questions or points:

1. What group of people do you speak of most highly in your life?
2. Be aware of the kind of positive language that you use to describe such people. Be mindful of the pleasant feelings, thoughts, and expressions that accompany your use of a positive stereotype.
3. Do you appreciate that others may have a negative stereotype of the same group of people? What is your response to their perceptions? Do you perceive any truth in other views?
4. What group of people do you find most difficult to accept? Do you belong to the culture of blame?
5. Be mindful of any negative stereotype that you hold of such people. Be aware that negative images are often influenced by the prevailing culture of the time (a century ago, for example, British colonialists and missionaries referred to the people of Africa as "savages").
6. Do you appreciate that other people speak highly of the group of people of whom you have a negative stereotype?
7. Are you able to express what you value about a group of people and, equally, what you feel concerned about?

Once we have recognized our own tendency to think in stereotypes it is much easier to overcome them. We can also accelerate this process by taking active steps to uncover the reality behind the images. Knowledge helps to dispel the ignorance that feeds the stereotype. If we felt ill-disposed toward Hindus, for example, we could arrange to be shown around a temple and to watch their acts of worship. We may find that witnessing the rituals at first hand gives us a real insight into a religious tradition other than our own, and sweeps away the reserve or disdain we may have previously felt.

Reading about the history and evolution of a nation or people can also help to shed light onto the darkness of our prejudice. To learn how Northern Ireland's troubles and the present-day conflict between Israelis and Palestinians are rooted in events of the past makes the motives, fears, and anger of all the sides involved more understandable. It then becomes less easy to write people off as "fanatics."

There are also important historical examples showing that bridge-building is effective in breaking down stereotypes. After World War II, elected officials in towns in Britain met with officials in towns in Germany to twin their respective towns to form new relationships. This twinning of towns took place throughout Europe. Through it, people were able to see their national stereotypes for what they were: simplistic distortions. Similarly, a few U.S. citizens have traveled to Japan, Vietnam, and Cuba to see for themselves states that have been hostile to their country. In years to come, Americans will no doubt visit places that are currently arenas of conflict, such as Afghanistan and Iraq. Again, such journeys help to break down stereotype images.

PROJECTING THE SHADOW

There is no greater proof of the challenge of working on ourselves than facing what has come to be known in psychotherapy as the "shadow." In one sense the word is used as a metaphor to describe the way past habitual tendencies dim the light of wisdom and clarity at the present moment.

Even with the best of intentions, many people find themselves facing a struggle, if not a war, of dark and light within themselves. It is the Jihad (Holy War) experienced by people trying to defeat problems and addictions bearing down on them. "I am my own worst enemy" is a phrase many of us use. The dark side of the inner life acts like a thunderstorm, blocking out the sunlight, even though the sun never stops shining.

In another sense, "shadow" is used particularly to describe the neglected parts of our lives—those aspects of our characters or personalities that we are perhaps ashamed of or deny or disown—which we then project onto others. So we might be habitually critical of those we think of as ambitious while being unaware of our own ambitiousness. Or we might have outspoken, highly aggressive views on gay liberation or women's rights because those movements stir an insecurity in ourselves that we are barely aware of at a conscious level.

To become aware of the shadow that we project helps us to understand both ourselves and others. To do this needs sensitivity, awareness, and courage, since confronting the darkness within is a challenging task. To do so, it might be helpful to consider the following:

1. Think about themes and topics that make us feel angry or upset out of all proportion.

2. Think about individuals whom we continually denigrate for certain qualities they have.

3. Make a list of things we are frightened of or hate, and try to be aware of people or groups who embody those fears and dislikes.

The way to deal with the shadow is to let as much light as possible into the dark recesses of our inner lives. Becoming aware is the first and hardest battle. Once we know what we have to deal with it becomes easier to see how our frailties color our thinking toward others. If we can then forgive ourselves for our failings, it becomes more manageable to withdraw our projections from others and "forgive" them for what we perceived as their special faults.

The problem of the shadow exists not only on a personal basis but also at a national level. As a society, we project our shadow in a general sort of way onto other groups and cultures and thereby end up denigrating, or even despising them. One of the most obvious contemporary examples of this syndrome can be seen with the West and the Arab world. Through countless news reports, too many of us in the West have come to suspect that Arabs and other Muslims universally advocate extremism. We view the Muslim faith as an alien religion instead of appreciating that its roots, just like those of Christianity, go back to the great Hebrew patriarch Abraham. We feel sure that the governments of all Arab nations are autocratic and uphold prejudice against women. Equally, there are Muslims who see the West in an equally distorted light. They see a society that is wholly and unredeemably godless and obsessed with materialism. They equate liberalism unequivocally with decadence. Our shadow feeds our stereotypical vision of them, and vice versa.

Through looking at these different views with spiritual awareness we can try to show the futility of taking sides in a violent confrontation. The Arab and the Western nations need to acknowledge the influence of the shadow upon their decision making and the way it fuels aggression, intolerance, and self-righteousness. Then it may be possible to see that what we blame others for doing exists to some extent in our own backyards. In this way Arabs may come to appreciate that, for example, materialism is not confined solely to the West. And the West may see that suppression of women and strict rules about dress are not exclusive to the Arab world. It is a matter of degree.

The following incident helps illustrate the point. One summer I made a pilgrimage with my companion, Nina, to climb and spend the night on Mount Sinai in Egypt, where Moses traditionally received the Ten Commandments. At the foot of the mountain, monks of the Greek Orthodox monastery of St. Catherine of Alexandria requested that pilgrims and tourists cover up their shoulders and legs as a mark of respect inside the sacred precincts. I noticed that one belligerent tourist began

protesting about having to conform to such protocol. He voiced his
stereotyped images of religion, but he forgot that his own secular culture
demands that men and women are expected to adopt a certain dress code.
What would happen to an office employee if he arrived at work wearing
only a pair of thongs, a huge sun hat, Hawaiian shorts, and a tank top on
a hot day? Secular culture has its own strict rules and pressures. It would
be fair to say that secular culture refuses to allow public or private sector
employers or employees to wear whatever they like to the office.

DEALING WITH PREJUDICE

There is an abundance of information, writings, and workshops dealing
with the variety of prejudices and stereotypes that run through society
and cause distress, and even terror. These tendencies take place not only
internationally but also in the workplace. Some people recognize that
their prejudices are deeply rooted and extend way back into childhood,
some of them unwittingly absorbed from parents. Yet, the same depth of
prejudice can also develop from perceptions and conclusions formed later
on in life and are often reinforced through contact with others who share
the same view.

More than fifty men were working on a building site in a provincial town
in England to modernize a school that had fallen into disrepair over many
years. Bricklayers, plumbers, painters, and electricians all joined together to
get the school finished. One day, a British painter of Caribbean descent,
walked into a toilet stall to continue his work when he came face to face
with a message painted on the wall: "You're not wanted in this country.
Get back you black bastard to where you came from." The distressed
painter told his supervisor, who immediately ordered other members of
the team to paint the obscene words out. No one owned up to the deed,
and the Caribbean man found himself speculating daily which of his fellow
workers had scrawled such an awful message.

People often have a perverse sense of loyalty to their own "group" that
breeds resentment and hatred toward another "group." We tend to

construct differences between people in our minds and then act on them. We often find this pattern arising in us despite the fact that we affirm intellectually that all forms of prejudice are unhealthy. Those who adhere to the principles of a multiracial and egalitarian society may find old emotions of prejudice arising when it involves personal matters, such as a family member entering into a mixed-race relationship, a rich person marrying a poor person, or a young adult starting a relationship with a much older person. The old stereotyped image finds its outlet and feeds doubts about, and anger toward, another person (whose behavior can also reinforce the old prejudice).

Once a prejudice has become established, it keeps arising in the foreground of consciousness. The Caribbean painter told me that one time a friend of his from the West Indies came to visit him in the town where he lived. When the two of them walked down the main street, some people looked the other way or even crossed the road. The two men felt unsure about the intentions of passersby, who were not used to seeing black people in the town.

Prejudice is like looking at the world through tinted glasses. If the prejudiced image arises in the mind, then that is what we see and remember. If we have only a limited understanding of diversity, we find ourselves identifying with those who are most like us and are unable to feel the same sense of closeness and intimacy with those who appear different. It is not easy to break out of this enclosed shell of existence, this old mental conditioning, and remain determined to go beyond appearances.

Our underlying fears uphold our prejudices, and this inhibits us from expressing concern or protest when we witness acts of discrimination. Our fear of speaking out strengthens the arrogance of those who portray a distorted view about others. Impressionable individuals then latch onto the stereotyping of people and imitate them. Gross generalizations, cynical views, and undermining jokes create an unchallenged culture of prejudice, indirectly supported by the silent fearful. The power of change comes when two types of people are willing to speak up: those on the receiving end of prejudice and those who see prejudice expressed by those of their own group, color, class, race, or the like.

It does not matter whether a person is in a position of authority or not, he or she must still deactivate the charged impressions that are projected onto another person or group. For example, if people who work together can meet to explore their attitudes toward one another, this will help to change the climate of their workplace. In a collective forum, those who usually feel inhibited to speak up may find the strength to voice their concerns. An active stance against any form of bias can release much goodwill and cooperation that serve the deeper interests of staff and company. In the story above, the works supervisor's strong support for the black painter made it easier for him to stay on the site. Also, he was helped by the fact that other workers came forward to support him.

Judiciary systems in Western societies have taken significant steps to challenge the prejudices and stereotyping that can destroy people's lives. But we have not yet started to extend these principles consistently on an international basis, using international law to protect people from pain brought about by prejudice. We are all one family. War is the external affirmation of internal forces of prejudice that seek to inflict suffering on others. Our society has not yet entered a debate about this. What we will not tolerate from our employers, we endorse in our leaders' treatment of people overseas. The only way to solve conflict is through constructive engagement. This will take a vision that requires a change in thinking. As people living on this earth, we have coexisted for far too long as a dysfunctional family. We have to take steps to heal divisions, address old wounds, and support each other through words and deeds.

CHALLENGING OUR PERCEPTIONS

People usually accept their perceptions as being true without questioning them. It seems that whatever our senses, feelings, and thoughts tell us, we believe. However, we rely far too much on what we see, hear, and remember, with all the various likes and dislikes that are involved. Our

STEPS TO ENDING OUR PREJUDICES

Overcoming prejudice is not something that happens overnight. We first need to build up an awareness of what our own personal prejudices are before we can tackle them. Some of them will be obvious to us, others will need a greater awareness. Use the following steps to help combat prejudice.

1. Make a genuine resolution to stop putting others down. Be aware, for instance, of a tendency to make disparaging or sarcastic remarks.

2. Acknowledge that making an enemy is a state of mind. Negative thinking will often lead to negative actions.

3. Transform the arrogance of superiority to awareness of interconnection. In the end, we are all subject to the human condition and need to help each other.

4. Become attuned to typical conditioned reactions and look for guidance and understanding from others to change your mind-set.

5. Listen to the kind inner voice rather than the hardened one. The positive voice may be submerged, but by being patient you will eventually hear it.

perceptions of ourselves, others, and events mostly happen at a very superficial level and take the same form, and most of us think they are carved in stone. At the same time, we tend to associate with people and things that reassure us in our perceptions and distance ourselves from those that threaten to upset our view of reality. We need the faith to doubt. In this regard, spiritual traditions and practice can help us to reconsider our habitual thinking about the world and so challenge our prejudices and stereotype images. An authentic spiritual view challenges the entire construction of our perceptions. This involves dismantling our tendency to make crude generalizations about people and, by extension, the mechanisms that lead to domestic and international conflict. All over the world, large numbers of people—ordinary men, women, and children— find themselves dragged into conflicts they have little appetite for. Instead of the opportunity to attend to their daily lives of work, leisure, relationships, and religious services, they become subjected to the decisions of heads of state and political/religious organizations. No wonder we often feel helpless and powerless to change the course of events. This sense of helplessness causes frustrations to grow and grow like a simmering volcano.

How perceptions can become fixed and destructive is shown by the following example. In July 2001, at one of two five-day Buddhist retreats I was leading at a kibbutz an hour's drive north of Tel Aviv, I spoke to a 40-year-old Tel Aviv woman office worker who expressed to me her suppressed anger and despair. "I want to kill every Palestinian. I wake up with this thought every morning. This is the only solution," she said.

"The final solution?" I asked.

"Yes, I know it is a terrible thing to say but this is what I am thinking every day." I had invited participants in the retreat to come to the front of the hall to inquire into anything that was affecting their lives. In a 40-minute dialogue, the woman and I made a dark journey into her inner world during which she pinned all the blame on the Palestinians. She seemed cynical about the hope and struggles for peace and reconciliation.

She may not have realized it but she had enough trust and confidence in herself to express her feelings, knowing full well that some people would be horrified at what they heard. This is the benefit of a spiritual retreat—it gives a sense of safety that allows people to share their deepest and darkest thoughts, to bring them into the light of awareness where they can dissolve. Although this woman was able to voice her dark perceptions about the situation in Israel and her violent solution to them, others suppressed them. I reminded the retreatants that such thoughts, expressed or unexpressed, appear in our everyday lives as pervasive resentment or sudden bursts of rage.

Some Israelis cried while listening to the session, others sobbed and left the hall—reflecting the feelings of helplessness ordinary Israelis harbor about changing their daily nightmare. As one participant said after the inquiry session: "Israel is falling apart. We have become a dysfunctional nation. We think things can't get worse but they do."

Despair and frustration haunt Israel, even among thoughtful people seeking to resolve the crisis. You cannot sit in a restaurant, walk the streets, get on a bus, or go to a club without thinking about terrorism. One day I was sitting having a cup of coffee in a crowded restaurant in Jerusalem when two Arab Israelis, one carrying a shopping bag, walked in to buy a drink. Some apprehensive customers watched the man closely when his hand went to his bag. Nothing happened ... this time.

Both Israelis and Palestinians are living through a hell in which their perceptions of each other have solidified, reinforcing prejudices. When this happens, dialogue is virtually impossible, because the perceptions block out the possibilities beneath the images they have fixed.

A spiritual approach can help to shake up entrenched mental and emotional positions and facilitate communication. Prayer, meditation, and reflection are the primary tools. They focus and still the mind, enabling us to go deeper within ourselves and realize a different way of being in the world, largely free from divisive views and negative reactivity. Through these practices we can:

1. Break the habit of seeing some people in either a purely positive or negative light. In doing this we recognize the nature of humanity, with all its diversity and complexity.

2. Challenge conventional perceptions and free up our minds. We hardly realize how much we have become imprisoned like birds in a cage by our perceptions of things.

3. Realize how much we rely on others in our lives—from lawyers and nurses to teachers and entertainers—and that we should resist projecting ingrained perceptions onto people we meet for the first time.

4. Realize that as human beings we share the same fears, terrors, and desires. Belonging to a particular group does not cancel our membership of the human race. We can strive toward acts of reconciliation rather than submit to the prejudices of our leaders.

FACTORS COMMON TO RELIGIONS

It is easy to fall into the habit of thinking that our own religion is the "best" one and that other believers have got it wrong. The following two lists show that religions, even from different cultural and historical backgrounds, have more in common—for good or for ill—than we may think.

POSITIVE FACTORS

1. Acts of compassion, service, and generosity.
2. Affirms moral basis for life.
3. Change through devotion, faith, meditation, realization, or revelation.
4. Enduring values—love, peace, justice.
5. Means for social change.
6. Recognition of community life.
7. Rituals pointing to "mysterium tremendum."
8. Support in the face of suffering.
9. Transcendence of cultural conditioning.
10. Points to the highest truth.

NEGATIVE FACTORS

1. Belief in the absolute authority of book, master, or tradition.
2. Belief in the superiority of a particular faith.
3. Discrimination against women.
4. Male hierarchical structures and privileges.
5. Lack of real appreciation of the sacredness of life.
6. Priority of nationalism before enduring religious values.
7. Promise of a Utopia—herein or hereafter.
8. Submissive, unquestioning obedience.
9. Support for wars and the political establishment.
10. Acts done in the name of God that produce suffering.

STEPS FROM ARROGANCE TO HUMILITY

Arrogance or a self-righteous attitude reveals itself through clinging to a particular viewpoint and a subsequent putting down of another's view of the same situation. The greater the arrogance, the greater the struggle to find a depth of mutual understanding between two parties involved in a conflict. There are several areas to examine if we find ourselves prone to arrogance.

1. Are we able to examine the consequences of clinging?
2. Are we able to see any weaknesses or contradictions in our argument?
3. Can we hear another point of view and see its strengths?
4. Do we experience any love or compassion in times of intense difficulties?
5. Do we perceive inner strength when there is humility or do we regard it as a sign of weakness?
6. Do we experience what we have in common with others, or do we hold to a superior position?

CHAPTER SIX

Cultivating Intimacy with Life

God's only command
When willing anything
Is saying to it "be!"
—and it is.
So glory to the one in whose hand
Is the dominion of all things
And to whom you will all be returned.

The Qur'an, Sura 36

I WAS DRINKING a cup of coffee in my local café in Totnes, Devon, when I spotted in a quiet corner of the shop two people sharing intimate moments together. It clearly looked like the beginning of a new relationship for them both, since they were sitting very close together, whispering, giving each other the fullness of attention. It was a sweet, romantic moment to observe.

We generally associate intimacy with the kind of close contact we have with a confidential friend. In spiritual language, intimacy goes much deeper than that. It expresses a depth of closeness that language cannot really communicate. What is the intimacy between an ocean, lake, or river and water? What is the intimacy that trees have with wood? What is the intimacy of milk blended with water?

The conventional forms of intimacy, such as two lovers sharing a coffee, may change. Their intimacy may be lost; they may become distant friends or even go their separate ways. But the intimacy between the ocean and water, trees and wood, remains unshakable. True spiritual awareness expresses the realization of this inseparable intimacy, no matter what happens.

To contemplate this deep sense of intimacy with life is an extraordinary undertaking and reaches out into every area of our existence. In times of conflict, we easily lose sight of this intimacy and fall into a divisive view of the world, our minds distracted by the painfulness of current events or by the pain of memories or fears for the future.

A spiritual perspective on life explores the significance of this intimacy and helps us realize that everything belongs to everything else, that everything affects everything else in an extraordinary fusion. In authentic intimacy with life, there is no flag to wave, no national anthem to proclaim, no belief that God is on our side. For God embraces all things. We demean God if we believe, even for a moment, that God takes sides. There is no fragmentation of the immeasurable. To be with God is to participate knowingly in the nondual expanse of things.

Yet even if we are not directly experiencing a national or international conflict, most of us are still far too habitually preoccupied with ourselves and what we want for ourselves and our immediate loved ones. There is a price to be paid for being self-indulgent in this way. It comes at the cost of a natural sense of oneness with life. By losing this, our thoughts and actions become charged with self-interest: "I," "me," and "mine" then take priority over all else.

At certain times it is easier to feel a natural intimacy with life. These times arise when, for example, we are taking a walk in the hills, swimming in the ocean, or experiencing the wonder of the night sky. These are important and precious moments. But they seem all too rare for most people. If we are to experience a natural intimacy with life, we have to change our values and priorities: we need to spend far more time experiencing a quiet intimacy with the most ordinary of tasks—from making a cup of tea to pulling weeds out of flower beds—as if it were our last day to experience life on Earth.

In a healthy relationship with life, we can be intimate with it in every moment, whether sitting on a train going to work, having a cup of coffee, or washing dishes after an evening meal. The capacity to forget ourselves, to let go of our self-indulgent attitudes, creates the receptivity that enables us to feel and know oneness. It is such a precious experience that it makes ownership and pursuit of material gain seem rather gross and superficial. That does not mean to say we can neglect our responsibilities and practical concerns. All of that belongs to the challenge of daily life. The exploration of oneness, of harmony with the immediate world, refines consciousness to the degree that we love the moments of life deeply.

To reconnect with life we need to explore the nature of intimacy—with ourselves, through memory and feelings; with other people; with our possessions; and with our feelings, beliefs, and opinions. By doing so we will perhaps uncover how our intimacy with life is hampered and blocked—for example by fear—and how we can restore ourselves to the sense of oneness that natural intimacy brings about.

Intimacy depends on love for its sustenance. Holding onto painful and wretched memories of people we have grown up with, known, or encountered can destroy our intimacy with them. Our heartache may prevent us from knowing whether it is fear, bitterness, or a desire to punish that motivates our decision to keep away from certain individuals, who may include those especially close to us, such as our parents. Conversely, intimacy can be renewed by the power of loving kindness. When this happens, healing can take place and prevent us from becoming prisoners to painful memories that would otherwise make us withdraw from others.

What are these memories that can make us captives and block out our capacity to feel intimacy? Memories are connected with time. They are feelings and images from the past that affect us in the present and influence the way we will act in the future. We can learn positive lessons from what we recall. Equally, we can find ourselves besieged with memories that torment our days and nights. If this occurs, we feel we are trapped by events that happened in the past. Yet locked into the view that time has these clear-cut divisions of past, present, and future, it may not even occur to us that there is no real past to go back to and examine. Our sense of time is something we impose on the world, forgetting that it is a mental construct and does not have absolute reality.

From a spiritual perspective, what we know and experience embraces totality in the here and now, in all of its grandeur and mystery. In witnessing the subtle depths of the here and now we can awaken to the ultimate truth, a steadfastness that is incorruptible and indestructible. This sublime presence remains unaffected by the changing face of time. It stands free from the mind's categories; it knows no past or future, no beginning or ending, no birth or death.

We can arrive in this timeless realm through meditation, by which all our mental activity can reach a state of utter silence, without a trace of a thought about the past, present, or future. Out of this palpable silence, the true nature of things emerges, free from marks, specific characteristics, and other features that determine the world of time and objects. Out of this profound experience spring insights that lay to rest our whole constructed world of time. We will also come to realize that death ceases to be an ultimate reality. The distinctive waves of the ocean of life easily spellbind our consciousness as they rise and fall, begin and end. Watching the waves coming into being then disappearing, we fail to witness the indestructibility of the water they are made of. The same indestructibility is true of the kingdom of God, which Jesus described as a "treasure in heaven that will not be exhausted, where no thief comes near, and no moth destroys. For where your treasure is, there your heart will be also." This realization is the refuge from all grief, sorrow, and terror.

Through meditation we can find the silence that returns us to our natural intimacy with life. It frees us from the destructiveness of painful memories that stay fixed inside our minds, locking us into the unchanging world of the past. Unable to break the chains of time, we are unable to break negative patterns of behavior. This was the experience of a man whose father possessed a terrible temper that frequently left him shivering with fear during his childhood. Although his father never physically abused his family, he would work himself up into an uncontrollable rage, yelling at his wife and their children. He never admitted to himself that he was the major problem in the household. Instead, he directed all blame toward his family, making their lives miserable, and refused to accept any criticism from anyone else. When he eventually left home, his son avoided all contact with him. Years later, however, he received an urgent message from his father asking him to visit him in their local hospital because he was dying from cancer. The son refused to go.

The son discussed the matter with his friends and other family members, who expressed various views but did not want to come down too strongly on one side or another. Again, his dying father appealed to him to come to the hospital. Again he refused. Some weeks later, the father died. A year later his son, who never found out why his father had often appealed to him to visit, claimed he had no regrets about staying away from him.

ATTENDING TO PAINFUL MEMORIES

It is possible for people to put the lid on painful past events, but there is no guarantee that pressure from within will not build up with unresolved personal history, forcing itself into the present, demanding attention and resolution. It is better to deal with the past than to ignore it or brush it aside. If you suffer from painful memories, ask yourself:

1. What exactly happened? What are the bare facts? What do I need to be clear about?
2. What are the most common feelings and thoughts surrounding the memory?
3. What is it that makes it most difficult?
4. Do I need someone to listen to these memories who I can trust won't also get caught up in them?
5. What do I need to be clear about as far as the past goes?
6. Have I indulged in memories for too long?
7. What has the past taught me?
8. Do I have to make the resolve today to move on from them?

This painful story reminds us how it is possible to lose contact even with someone who shares our own flesh and blood. We may not know what it is like to live in a household with an angry father but most of us would have liked the son to have found enough love within himself to agree to his father's request. We feel that the father who was dying may have had regrets about his past behavior—that he had changed inwardly and wanted to reconcile himself with his son before death. We may feel that the son lacked a generosity of spirit and was clinging to painful memories. It seems he did not consider whether his father had undergone a change of heart. Yet we should resist being too judgmental. After all, the son had no idea of his father's intention for calling him to his bedside. Perhaps he did not wish to rake over the coals of the past. We can only speculate. Yet in the spiritual life it would be fair to say that the general principle, but not an absolute rule, is to take risks for healing and wholeness.

FREEDOM FROM FEAR

Many people take a hot shower every morning before going off to work. On reaching the end of the hot shower, there is the opportunity to invigorate the body by turning on the cold water. The first fear of the day may arise at this point in time. Although cold water will not cause any harm, the mind resists the experience, afraid to feel the sudden rush of cold on the skin, and perhaps desires a gradual shift to warm or cool water. In the same sort of way, many of us are frightened to experience a direct contact with intimacy. And this fear can become a habit, preventing us from becoming fully intimate with life. Fear, in short, is the mind's reaction to a possible future event based on memory of the past.

Some claim that fear is a vital human instinct. But fear blocks wise action, inhibits our capacity to take steps forward, generates reactivity instead of calm appraisal, and inhibits the capacity to deal with situations in an appropriate way. A single painful situation can imbed itself in a person's mind and have a long-term impact on their life with no guarantee of a full recovery. When people are or feel under attack or besieged, either

The key to overcoming fear in all its forms and to developing intimacy is the practice and application of mindfulness throughout the day. Through mindfulness we learn a lot about ourselves, including how much the mind wanders, and the range of fears, anxieties, thoughts, ideas, and images that overshadow immediate reality. As our mindfulness deepens, we experience a deep inner peace and a greater connectedness with the present via our eyes, ears, nose, tongue, and touch. We find we engage with life much more, and so place fewer demands on ourselves and others or feel the need for bigger and more expensive possessions. Mindfulness helps to open up and expand our inner lives.

• When waking up in the morning, be aware that everything matters in the light of mindfulness.
• When sitting down, be mindful of what you are sitting on and of your posture.
• When walking, be mindful of each step you take, of how fast or slow you are going, whether or not you swing your arms.
• When eating, be mindful of your food, whether it is salty or sweet or spicy, its texture, the speed with which you eat it.
• When conversing, be mindful of the words you are saying and the thoughts that arise as you speak or listen to someone else.

physically or mentally, they can be deeply affected by the constant atmosphere of intimidation, of not knowing what comes next. With abusers in control of their lives, the abused feel lonely and alienated. They lose their sense of intimacy with those around them as well as the power to love and to experience peace of mind. And, deprived of love as a foundation for action, they can find their sense of worth altered to the extent that even close friends and family will hardly recognize them. It is only through cultivating a climate of intimate support through love, care, and respect for those who are desperately unhappy, that we can help them to allow their broken hearts to heal.

The unresolved emotional problems of individuals can play havoc in their lives. A wife regularly abused by her husband after his drinking sessions can feel unexpected terror whenever she hears the slamming of a door or sees a violent movie on television. Those who have been involved in an aircraft crash or serious incident may feel a sense of panic on hearing a plane flying overhead. People who have been burglarized may feel fear whenever they hear a sudden noise outside in the street.

Fear can also have a powerful effect at a collective level. As a nation, we can be filled with a range of fears and anxiety when a powerful state historically inimical to our own nation embarks on carrying out military exercises. As a race, we can feel similar emotions when scientists warn us of global warming and the melting of the polar ice cap and the subsequent rise of the seas and oceans.

The point about these and other fears, both at the personal and collective levels, is that they block our ability to respond to the present, the here and now, and so live our lives in fullness.

They can undermine or destroy our sense of worth, and distort our feelings, thoughts, speech, and actions in a negative way. In doing so they break the bonds of natural intimacy that connect us to others. Spiritual practice teaches us to act wisely in the face of personal and global situations.

There is a limit to what our senses can know and what our minds can reveal about another person. It is rare that our minds act as empty vehicles and pick up what another person experiences. This begs the question as to whether we can ever actually come to know anybody, since we cannot know the exact experiences of another. Nevertheless, although we may not know others, it is possible for us to feel a depth of love and appreciation for others.

We determine the value of individuals by the way they behave in the world, which means relying on what they do, say, or write. This reveals only the outer expression of their lives, nothing more. We draw conclusions about them based on our limited perceptions and sensory knowledge. We may find ourselves in general agreement with others about certain people. Also, if we tell people directly what we feel about them our perceptions may seem distorted or inaccurate—they may agree or disagree completely with our appraisal, or agree with some of our perceptions and disagree with other points. Who is right? We have to acknowledge that in the final analysis, we cannot see another person's experience in any absolute way. Our perceptions of others, and their perceptions of us, can be summarized by the following statements:

• I do not know what your experience is of a situation.

• You cannot know my experience of a situation.

• I do not know what your experience is of me.

• You cannot know my experience of you.

• I do not know your experience of yourself.

• You do not know my experience of myself.

If by some miracle we were able to know each other it would probably help us all to understand each other's lives a lot better and achieve a degree of mutual intimacy. But we do not. Since we lack this vital knowledge, we end up groping around trying to understand each other, trying to make sense of each other. In the face of such realities, we struggle to get along with one another as best we can.

transforming our terror

REFLECTING ON INTIMACY WITH OTHERS

Wisdom reminds us that I cannot know your experience of me, and I cannot know my experience of you—I can only test it by reflecting it back to you in words to see how much I have understood you. You can do the same for me. If we listen to each other, we may be able to heal the wounds in a painful relationship. Reflect upon the following thoughts with the hope that they may lead to wise actions that express natural intimacy and an abiding unity with all that coexists.

• Let me reflect on what I have in common with those I know.

• Let me reflect on what I have in common with those who live far away.

• Let me reflect on what I have in common with the rest of life.

• Let me reflect on what we all share together instead of constantly dwelling on differences.

• Let me reflect on the fact that others do not want to suffer, just as I do not.

• Let me reflect on the fact that others want to be happy, just as I do.

• Let me reflect on the fact that others want to live in peace and security, just as I do.

It is love that makes intimacy possible on a sustained basis. If we cannot tolerate the perceived behavior of another, then it is likely to affect our subsequent behavior toward them. This means that if we are not in touch with one another the gap between us will widen: your experience remains hidden from me and my experience remains hidden from you, and so we are dependent on our inferences as the yardstick for what we say or do in response to one another.

The members of a nongovernment organization in India found themselves subjected to a malicious rumor campaign. Speculation that members of the organization were involved in illegal activities, making pornographic videos, and molesting children was widely repeated. There was no basis for any of the rumors, but an independent investigation was required for the rumors to be refuted. The report was filed only after a great deal of distress had been caused to the organization's members and a lot of their time had been wasted. One member said: "We would rather have spent the time working for the poorest of the poor."

Our behavior toward others far too often depends upon their behavior toward us. In a destructive cycle, both parties behave similarly until one party or the other agrees to stop. There is no limit to the degree of suffering that can arise before reaching that point. Equally, there is no limit to the expressions of love and intimacy that we can share with others, near or far, even including offering our lives to others. Love and constructive engagement need a true freedom of spirit. We say we will change when they change; and some believe the only means of breaking this cycle is by destroying the other. On a global level, this could continue until everybody has exterminated everyone else. "We will carry on until you stop" has a merciless rationality to it.

INTIMACY WITH THE WORLD OF THINGS

Ownership can become a warped way of finding intimacy with the world. We feel that if we own something, such as a house or some luxury good, then we become more intimate with it. This attitude shows mental confusion. Clinging to the idea of ownership sustains alienation: as we indulge our feelings on what we possess, we become more alienated from everything else. One of the most powerful comments on the culture of ownership has been expressed in a Cree Indian prophecy:

> *Only after the last tree has been cut down,*
> *Only after the last river has been poisoned,*
> *Only after the last fish has been caught,*
> *Only then will you find that money cannot be eaten.*

If we can treat our relationship with our possessions or our desire for them sensibly and put it in due proportion, we can develop a greater intimacy with all aspects of life, including our brothers and sisters everywhere on this Earth.

I remember as a young boy visiting the home of a school friend about the same age as myself. As soon as I entered his home, I became aware of how impeccably clean and tidy it was. We were not allowed in through the front door but only the back one. There was not a thing out of place. My friend's mother watched the two of us like a hawk as we played a game together in what was a very stilted atmosphere. I did not stay long and was glad to leave.

Our obsession with and attachment to things and appearances destroy our sense of being at ease with our surroundings. A healthy attitude will allow for both tidiness and untidiness, order and disorder, and for, say, doing the dishes on the following day rather than right away. My friend and his mother seemed to be prisoners in their own home.

It is very easy to confuse identification with material things with intimacy with them. At times, we may need to remind ourselves that real intimacy implies that everything interacts with everything else in a dimension of wholeness. The ego can easily slip into identifying itself with material goods through its belief in possession and ownership instead of connection and intimacy. An elderly grandfather had devoted many hours since he was

QUESTIONING OUR POSSESSIONS

We are in danger of losing our intimacy with life if we become obsessed with wealth. To break out of our fetish with money and goods, we have to be willing to break the grip of the consumer culture that prevails in our society. Otherwise we will live as slaves to the material world. Think about the following questions and use them to focus on your relationship to property and goods.

1. Do I define myself by what I own—for instance my house or automobile?

2. How would I spend my energy and time if I had no interest in consumer goods?

3. What would I do if I only had a year to live—would I focus on accumulating material wealth?

4. What are the things in my life that are more important than being a consumer? How do they manifest themselves?

5. How would I feel if a material object dear to me were to be destroyed?

6. If my house was burning down, what things would I want to try to save first?

a teenager to collecting stamps from around the world. He had become something of an expert in stamp collecting. One day he came to the decision that it was time to pass on some of his albums to his grandson, also an avid stamp collector. After a few months, however, the grandfather began to miss his albums—eventually to the extent that his wife had to ask her grandson for their return. It left the grandson depressed for weeks. He felt he was not trusted with his grandfather's albums.

The grandfather's clinging to his collection and fear of loss destroyed the spirit of openness, the sense of interconnection (between him and his grandson), and the expansive awareness that are the hallmarks of authentic intimacy. The grandfather's ego wanted to stay in control of his stamp collection. The result was that his clinging became a rigid substitute for a passionate but fluid relationship with his stamps. Believing that he was losing his stamp collection, he felt panic.

INTIMACY WITH OUR INNER LIVES

If our lives lack vision or direction, we become liable to grasp at situations that give us a feeling of self-importance. We, or politicians acting on our behalf, may seize upon a conflict to provide a sense of power. Then, having committed ourselves to aggressive action, we find we do not know how to stop. We and our opponents attack each other in what becomes a savage spiral. To sustain this situation, both parties enter into denial about the breadth and depth of the harm they are causing. Until we truly become fully conscious human beings, willing to examine ourselves, we will not find solutions to major problems between us. Instead, we will carry on much as before. So, we have a moral imperative to be self-critical, to look into our souls, and not simply indulge in criticizing others.

Soul-searching shows a willingness to look within, no matter how uncomfortable the experience. It is not a matter of laying blame upon ourselves or drumming up guilt and anguish for past deeds. But it does mean being willing to open our hearts to others' concerns or accusations so that we find the commitment to make amends and develop a level of understanding between them and us. We will then show sensitivity or restraint around events in the future.

The process of soul-searching starts with the individual. I received a series of e-mails from a close friend, an unusual European woman in her mid-30s, who was going through a deep spiritual crisis. Losing her direction in life, she had ended a deep and loving relationship with her partner and lost interest in her vision to serve Mother Earth. In her e-mails she wrote: "My life is passing by. I feel I have wasted so much time." She also told me on the phone that her friends found it difficult to make sense of her crisis. After all, she liked her job; she owned an apartment that had a modest mortgage; she had natural good looks, many friends, and good relationships with her family. What was she so concerned about?

In such times of personal existential terror there are no immediate answers. Powerless at such a time, the self can do little but travel along with the uncertain journey of the inner life. I told her that hopefully a sudden insight or some deep experience or conversation would enable her to put her mind at rest. She must be patient and allow her crisis to be resolved naturally as well as listen to the wisdom of another person who understands her crisis.

From her later e-mails, there seemed to be no let-up as she struggled day in and day out with existential questions as to whether life had any meaning, direction, or purpose. She had lost weight. She disliked her own company. She felt the need to break out of the oppressive constraints of her life and said that when she started to let go she felt excitement, "the pain, the sorrow, the love, and the wonder." At times, she said that she felt very close to comprehending her process, but then doubts would occur. Her painful, transformative experience reminded me of a famous statement in the Buddhist tradition that is as relevant today as it ever was:

Great Doubt: Great Awakening.
Little Doubt: Little Awakening.
No Doubt: No Awakening.

Such words remind those struggling to make sense of life that they are not alone. Others, past and present, have been willing to make this journey into the unknown without any assurance that such a crisis will lead anywhere. To her credit, the woman was willing to expose herself to the forces of her inner world while staying in touch with the incomprehensible nature of life. Those who settle for career, order, and the so-called "good life" may never embark on her journey.

Soul-searching is a process that heals the past and allows the forces of kindness and wisdom to be expressed in the future. It does not matter whether the process is facilitated by a conversation with a friend, a particular religion, or the skills of counselors. What is important is that transformation occurs. A major catastrophe gives us the opportunity to inquire into our relationship with our beliefs, feelings, and opinions, and it also acts as a metaphor for other situations where there is conflict and a seemingly insoluble position. From a spiritual standpoint, there are certain questions that need to be addressed if we are going to break the patterns affecting our way of looking at events. They include:

1 | AM I LIVING IN FEAR AND DISTRUST?

If so, what am I willing to do to make changes? Our state of mind becomes a critical factor in the way we respond to events. We ignore the fact that our experiences are subjective and fool ourselves into thinking that we know objective reality. In any important exploration of conflict, whether on a large or domestic scale, we need to acknowledge that our feelings, thoughts, and perceptions are factors that contribute to the whole view. The attitude of the commentator is bound to influence the commentary: the observer gives substance to the observed. So the tone of any communication we have needs to be prefaced by "I believe that they are ..." rather than simply "They are ..." We need to remain open to all possibilities. If we are inflexible, we ignore changes of heart or appropriate responses by the other party since it would mean us having to change our attitude or strategy.

Feelings of empathy matter a great deal. There is little point in saying "Yes, I feel for the plight of others" if our underlying attitude means that we continue in the same old way. Empathy and compassion signify solidarity with the plight of others. It is this kind of response that moves our hearts toward acts of reconciliation and toward sustaining the effort to overcome the forces that inflict suffering on others. We can be determined to develop loving kindness toward all those who suffer; and to break out of the trap of being in a "for and against" position and adopt a different approach to notions of victory and defeat. This determination points the way to non-dual realization.

3 | CAN I BE EVENHANDED IN A DISPUTE?

In a dispute, there are four basic positions that I can adopt. They are to:

1) criticize both sides;

2) ignore both sides;

3) support one side against the other;

4) support both sides.

Our feelings and tendencies will influence which of the four stances we take. At times, we must use our critical faculties skillfully and dare to voice what we believe deserves examination. Our hearts may often feel more sympathetic to one party or the other, but this bias says more about our feelings than external facts. It is usually easier to engage in a polemic against one side rather than the other—the challenge is to pinpoint neutrally the various conditions causing suffering to either party. Impartial perceptions impress with their aware, balanced, and intimate understanding of suffering and how to resolve it.

In cases of violent conflict, our immediate response to killing and retaliation is either to condemn or support it based on our view of what is right and wrong. The constant denouncing of others escalates the divisions even further. Deep down, we know that things do not have to be this way. Deep inquiry will make it clear that taking sides, and the constant craving for victory, shows a neurotic dependency on the self and its beliefs. Knowing it is possible to collapse these psychological walls creates a power that defies the conventional world with its clinging to power and desire for control over results.

4 | DO I BELIEVE THAT THE ENDS JUSTIFY THE MEANS?

We need to be sure that we examine means and ends impartially. We target a particularly desirable goal that seems achievable at a certain point in the future. After embarking on a particular course of action, we feel the momentum building up. As time passes, the means often become a way of life, while the end remains far off, a distant dream. At this point, we find that we have to keep justifying the means because of the time, energy, and resources we have devoted to them.

Initially we may be convinced that there is a close tie-in between a particular means and end, and we can all too easily maintain that conviction despite the fact that it becomes apparent to outsiders that they bear little relationship to each other. So we need to monitor our attitude toward means and ends carefully. If we find that we are gaining substantial benefit from the means we should acknowledge it as a warning sign and examine our motives. And if we then find that the means are self-serving and unlikely to achieve their intended end we need to have the courage to change or halt the process.

❖ ❖ ❖

MEDITATION ON TREATING OTHERS
AS WE WISH TO BE TREATED

To treat others as we wish to be treated, we have to apply this spiritual ethic to all without exception. When we do not hold any anger, hatred, or desire to retaliate, we have realized what oneness means at the deepest level. The words of the following meditation may be read quietly or spoken aloud. They are intended to induce a sense that we all share this Earth.

• Let me stop perceiving the differences between others and myself
So that I neither applaud my position, nor condemn the standpoint of others. For they have done that for so long and so have I.

• I know not who started making these differences so significant.
Perhaps they did, and now I start doing the same,
Perhaps I did, and now they start doing the same.
Perhaps we started together, not knowing
Whether the seed or the fruit came first.

• Let me put aside the differences
So they become surmountable and so I can dwell
On what is in common.
I am born, I age, I experience pain. I die. So do they.

• There are people in my life whom I love
And people who are difficult, sometimes to the extreme.
There are people who will listen and those who resist.
I know it is the same for them,
Whoever they are, wherever they are.

• I wish to be treated with respect, to be understood and heard.
May I treat others as I wish to be treated.
For then we can move forward. Together.

CHAPTER SEVEN

Dealing with Authority and its Abuse

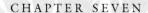

In the name of God,

The compassionate and the merciful,

Sovereign of the day of judgment

You alone we worship,

And to you alone we turn for help.

Guide us to the straight path.

The Exordium from the Qur'an

THE WORLD IS a small place in which it is all too easy to be aware of countless examples of abuse of authority. Governments, religious authorities, violent political groups, and powerful organizations impose their will on ordinary people, who struggle to stop the exploitation of their lives and their environment. It is hard to stand up to these various forces, which at times can seem so formidable. Yet spiritual awareness calls upon us to bring a moral concern to these major arenas of life. We need to use all our strength and independence to examine the way the authoritarian shadow falls upon us. Like trying to see the lines of a hand very close to your face, it can be difficult to see the imposition of questionable authority on your life at home. You need to hold the hand away to see its lines properly.

The various ways in which authorities influence our lives are not always easy to pick out. But if, say, we felt that our government was manipulating public opinion to support its version of reality, what would be an appropriate way for us to respond? Sensing the misuse of power, we would either have to challenge the government's authority or remain passive.

If, however, we decided that we were not going to live as poor, downtrodden creatures, paying lip service to authority, we have the potential to express what is called in the spiritual tradition of the East the "original mind." Instead of blindly repeating what we have been told to believe, we experience and acknowledge our doubts, even if this proves to be uncomfortable.

By doing this, we cultivate the original mind; and our moral authority is then revealed in our capacity to think for ourselves rather than acting like obedient children submitting to a powerful parent.

While our political leaders feed us selective information to communicate a certain position, the original mind is able to realize a deep intimacy with what lies behind all the slogans, labels, and images; and it feels a depth of love for all those who suffer and the need for commitment to constructive engagement to resolve great problems. Not surprisingly, this spiritually informed attitude is not something most heads of state care for in their concern to win over their citizens with their political rhetoric.

Yet, there is a place for wise authority in life. We need to be clear about its features so that we can distinguish it from an abusive form of authority driven by the need for power. A true authority expresses a wise and compassionate approach to human problems. It shows a genuinely sustainable, nondivisive view and it understands the deeper viewpoints of those who disagree violently with its position. A true authority is willing to be constructive with adversaries and speak openly about past and present misunderstandings, exploitation, and suffering; and it reveals a wise and mature response to events rather than a retaliatory one. If we can recognize those qualities in an authority, we have the grounds to place our faith in it. Wise leadership has the inner power to acknowledge mistakes of the past in matters of policy and perception as well as in the determination not to repeat history. In spiritual terms, this means ending the old "karma" and creating causes and conditions for healing and wholeness.

To bring a sense of moral concern to our lives we need to understand the use and abuse of authority and to explore the ways in which authority manifests itself, especially in the crucial arenas of religion, war, and politics, and also how abuse operates in us at a personal level. By increasing our awareness we can respond effectively to abusive authority from a spiritual perspective.

INJUSTICE IN THE NAME OF RELIGION

There have been countless wars and other conflicts throughout the history of mankind, and it is a sad truth that some of them have been fought under the banners of God and religion. To an impartial observer, it would seem that God's revelation includes massacres and despotic wars. Today, leaders of major religions continue to defend the so-called "just war" and give assurance that there is no sin in bombing, shooting, or attacking enemies. Priests, mullahs, and rabbis tell militants and soldiers that killing their enemies—including political targets, soldiers, and civilians—in war is

different from murder. Having accepted the authority of their religious
leaders, believers go off feeling assured that if they die for their cause, their
souls will go heaven.

Going to war in the belief that it is the will of God is something common
to most, if not all, religions and cultures in history. And it is easy to see
that present-day conflicts and suffering clearly have parallels with those of
the past. It has been said that if we do not learn from history we are
doomed to repeat it. By studying the past we can see how war tends to
arise in similar ways. For example, Jerusalem has seethed with conflict off
and on for around a hundred generations, with claims and counterclaims
by various peoples for control over the city. Today, there seems to be little
hope in sight for reconciliation, because of the belligerence and demands
of the opposing sides.

In fact we are left wondering whether any people in the region (or in
more recent times the international community) has made any progress
toward resolving these religious and political disputes, which have rumbled
on since the Middle Ages and before. During the 11th century C.E., the
principal rulers in Europe no longer perceived the Vikings as a threat to
their security and moved toward seeing the Muslims as the new force to
be feared. This perception contributed to the Crusading movement, which
lasted for about 200 years. To encourage the Christian soldiers and knights
to undertake these military expeditions to the Holy Land against the
Muslims, the Church promised them that penance due to sin would be
remitted. Also, if they died in battle they would be rewarded with a
martyr's crown, allowing them to go straight to heaven. So the Christian
armies who set out for the Holy Land were bolstered by religious authority
and the prospect of divine reward, just as Muslim suicide attackers are
today. But using God as an excuse to kill enemies cannot be justified
whatever the religion. God demands love, compassion, and justice from us,
not slaughter.

Religious authority is conducted through hierarchical structures. It also
receives crucial backing from sacred texts, which have a particularly

significant place in Judaism, Christianity, and Islam. In fact it was because Jews and Christians were "people of the book" that Muslims treated those of them who lived in Islamic lands with a certain degree of respect and toleration—which was not reciprocated to Muslims in European lands.

Sacred texts, such as the Qur'an and the Bible, have been an extraordinary source of inspiration. For many deeply religious people, however, it is easy to see the great merit of their own scriptures and hard to accept the validity of those of other religions. Yet, as with other forms of authority, we have to use discerning judgment with sacred texts, focus on those passages that uphold deep values, show love and compassion, and point to the presence of God or truth in the midst of things.

For if we are not careful, we can easily become selective in the way we read a holy book. For example, the issue of a respected New York Buddhist magazine that followed September 11 published Buddhist responses to the conflict. A prominent Buddhist writer picked out some passages from the Qur'an that he described as a "sobering experience." He said the "text keeps returning to the divisive and warlike language of 'us' versus 'them'," and he referred to the book's "implicit incitement to violence." In the following issue of the same magazine, a lecturer in Arabic language at New York University described (rightly in my view) that the Buddhist writer had engaged in a "highly selective reading" of the Qur'an and thus did not do "justice to the complexity and richness of its message."

In the same way, it would be easy to take passages from the Bible that would also be a "sobering experience"—for example, the divine destruction of Sodom and Gomorrah or the killing of the firstborn sons of Egypt before the exodus of the Israelites. We feel similar concern about apparently inflammatory statements in the Hindu holy book, the Bhagavad Gita, when God incarnated in the form of Krishna encourages Arjuna to kill his enemies on the battlefield—since Krishna claims that those who die will be reborn. Yet if we dismissed the Bible, the Bhagavad Gita, and the Qur'an on the basis of difficult passages, we would miss the complexity and richness of the deep spiritual teachings in their pages.

We must not forget that words on paper lack inherent significance. They lack the power to force men and women to behave in any particular way. We attribute authority to a particular book, but it patently lacks it. The Qur'an and other sacred texts remind us to leave everything in the hands of God. We need to read passages from them that emphasize the importance of love, compassion, and justice. Our world would be a poorer place without sacred literature, despite the anomalies, that challenges our secular culture with discerning passages of wisdom and love.

AWARENESS OF RELIGIOUS AUTHORITY

How aware are we of the extent religious authorities have played and continue to play in our lives? Do we feel at ease with them? Do we dare to challenge them? The following questions are intended to help us explore our relationship with God, religion, and the holy scriptures.

• Have we been brought up to believe in God and the holy scriptures being the ultimate authority?

• Are our actions influenced by a religious authority and in what way?

• How do we react to those whose religious authority differs from our own?

• What happens to our state of mind when we read a sacred book? Do we appreciate that the mind alone takes words on paper and reifies them or makes them real?

• Do we believe that we all belong to God or the expanse of Life?

• Do we imagine that God favors one side over another in a conflict?

• Have we ever witnessed people threaten others in the name of God? How did we react?

Apart from other sensitivities about war, there are many religious people who question the assurance of heaven for those who die for a "just war." In the Buddhist tradition there is the story of a professional soldier who found himself engaged in intensive soul-searching. Deeply concerned about his involvement in killing and wounding others on the battlefield, he went off to talk to the Buddha. He confided in him that his religious leaders had told him that if he died in battle, he would go to heaven. However, he experienced doubts about their authority.

"What do you say about that?" he asked the Buddha. The Buddha seemed reluctant to answer his question. The soldier must have sensed that what the Buddha was about to say would be painful to hear. Nevertheless, he insisted that the Buddha speak and asked him the same question three times.

Looking at him directly, the Buddha said that those who strive in war already have a mind that is "low, depraved, and misdirected." He then added that those who slaughter people show an utter misunderstanding of the way to heaven. "Upon dying in a battle, the soldier will find himself in hell," the Buddha added. The soldier burst into tears. The Buddha said he knew this would be very distressing to hear, which is why he had hesitated to say anything.

"I'm not crying because of what you said," replied the soldier, "but because I have been deceived for so long by other soldiers and religious leaders, who told me I would go to heaven if I died fighting." The Buddha stated emphatically that dealing in arms was utterly incompatible with the spiritual life.

According to the Buddha, from a spiritual perspective, war cannot be just. Every time we support decisions that inflict suffering on other people, we rob them of their intrinsic worth as human beings. Our stance not only tells us about the unresolved forces within us that condone naked aggression, but also reveals our lack of faith in dialogue, that remarkable feature of our species that enables resolution of terror through language.

It is dialogue, the skillful use of words, which ensures a true encounter with others. For language seeks to meet others rather than destroy them. It is this capacity to describe what we feel and think in front of others that paves the way for the resolution of difficulties. We can discuss and negotiate agreements, and it is in our refusal to listen and support others that we sow the seeds for violence—a violence that can explode on the innocent.

Whether these acts of violence come from personal rage or from acting under the orders of others, their impact and consequences remain the same. It is the suffering they bring about that counts, as well as the factors that created them. We make war to impose our version of truth ruthlessly upon others, as if they had no right to dispute our view of reality. Both sides refer to each other as evil, believing they themselves are on the side of good. Both sides refuse to examine the causes and conditions for conflict that have become obscured by these charged and destructive concepts.

Yet, we are faced with an imperative to examine the range of reasons for violence without justifying one set of conditions and refuting another. Through a balanced investigation, there is the potential for a meaningful exchange and the chance to transform suffering. The basis for this exchange is through understanding that others wish to live free from suffering as much as we do. By making this inner shift we are able to see beyond the loyalties and bias of the self and look with the eyes of God, with the eyes of mercy and compassion for everyone.

Few men and women engage in truly despotic acts of cruelty. This is true even of soldiers, who are trained to commit acts of violence—it would be unfair to categorize those in the armed services as living out psychotic impulses to kill and maim others. However, even if an army psychologist pronounced the minds of certain combat forces to be psychologically and emotionally healthy, it is the condition of the mind that obeys all orders that is of the greatest concern to those investigating the nature of freedom. The first rule in the armed services is unquestioning obedience to superiors. Trained in such a way, military personnel follow orders without examining the basis for them; and those who question their political leaders face severe retribution.

This issue of obeying orders unquestioningly was brought home to me during a public talk I recently gave in a synagogue in Tel Aviv, Israel. At one point I asked the audience to tell their fathers, brothers, sons, and uncles to put down their rifles and to refuse to drive tanks or fly helicopters in the occupied territories that belonged to their neighbors, the Palestinians. Three men walked out when I made this appeal. To refuse to engage in threatening and intimidating action, let alone in killing people, is an act of inner freedom. Those brave enough to resist the orders of their superiors to cause suffering reveal a spiritual awareness and an attitude to authority that transcends the dominant view.

After the talk, a young man came up to me and said: "I am a combat soldier with the IDF [Israeli Defense Force]. I realize we have no right to engage in collective punishment of the Palestinian people in this way." Then he added: "More and more young Israelis are refusing conscription. I shall not step again into Palestine as a soldier. The authorities will probably send me to prison for a couple of months for disobeying orders. It is not easy. My wife is pregnant and is expecting a baby soon."

I believe young men like him are a credit to themselves, their families, and their country for refusing to make war on others. These soldiers have to put up with hardship and verbal abuse from their peers and seniors in refusing to surrender to the demands of the nation-state. It is in such confrontation that men and women test their mettle as to whether they can treat others as they wish to be treated. As a governing principle, this great ethic for human existence reveals a noble way of life.

❖ ❖ ❖

REFLECTING ON CONFLICT

How do we feel personally about war and conflict? What would we ask ourselves if, for example, another or others attacked us in one form or another? Our questions might include:

1. What are their motives? Why are they very hostile toward us and seek to harm us? What is it they do not understand?
To start with, we have to look very carefully and honestly at the situation as we try to fathom as openly as possible what is going on.

2. What do they want? What do they hope to achieve through their words or actions?
It often becomes apparent to us that the means people use to get their way may bring about the complete opposite of what they really want. Spellbound in ignorance, the mind fails to see the painful karma it sows through lack of wisdom about means and ends.

3. Do I have any responsibilities, directly or indirectly, in this issue? What are they? Have I said or done anything that has triggered such a response?
We may have to take a good, long, hard look at ourselves to see if we have created difficulties or contributed to the suffering, either actively or through neglect.

4. Am I willing to try to resolve the problem?
In soul-searching, this is often one of the hardest questions to produce a positive response to. We may need to apologize, make amends, show compassion, and be willing to admit we have made mistakes or have ignored the anguish of others. We also need the courage to realize that this open attitude may mean having to defy an authority, but that it is necessary for our spiritual health.

STRIFE AND TRADITION

Many of the conflicts in the world, past and present, have been due to ethnic strife, when two races or communities, historically divided by culture, traditions, or religious beliefs, have fought each other with a determination hardened by time. Apart from the situation in the Middle East, we only have to think of the constant tensions and hostilities, sometimes sporadic, sometimes protracted, between Sinhalese and Tamils in Sri Lanka, Indians and Pakistanis over Kashmir, Protestant Loyalists and Catholic Republicans in Northern Ireland, and Serbs, Croats, and Muslims in former Yugoslavia. What are the roots of these conflicts? What causes such deep and violent divisions between people? From a spiritual perspective the search for an answer begins with the self and others. Our ignorance of ourselves and tendency to build ourselves up at the expense of others are the building blocks on which larger conflicts are raised. To understand aggression between two sides, therefore, we need to first look at ourselves and our standpoints.

In the Buddhist tradition, practitioners of awareness and self-understanding examine projections either onto themselves or others. These projections become layers covering basic reality. Buddhists have wisely stated that ignorance propels the tendencies to cause harm. Under the sway of ignorance, we think that ignorance belongs to others, as though we had exclusive rights to true knowledge and understanding. If a change is to take place in our relationships, we have to acknowledge our blind spots and our areas of ignorance before we project such failings onto others. We have to understand the force of history as well as contemporary pressures. By admitting ignorance we pave the way for humility and willingness to engage in those things that support the deeper interest of all.

For the self to inflict suffering in the name of a belief, it needs some kind of authority to substantiate what it does. This authority often takes strength from historical precedence for support. Without drawing on history and beliefs, the self would feel incapable of acting in destructive ways on its own. Since the essential nature of the self is empty of substance, it needs the force of the past, personal, and historical to inject itself with authority to support a cause greater that itself. In the eyes of the self, the nation, or the religion, beliefs give credence to the application of terror or the initiation of war. The self then appoints itself as the lord over life and death.

But when the self does not cling to its traditional authority in a dogmatic way and nurtures tolerance, it can promote a similarly relaxed outlook in others. This is illustrated by the following story told between Muslims and Jews. It reveals the goodwill that used to exist between the two communities. Centuries ago, the mullah in Damascus had a very sore throat, so he was unable to chant the opening words of the Qur'an from the top of his minaret to the faithful below. He knew that his neighbor, a rabbi, had a strong voice, so he asked him if he would kindly climb the steps of the minaret and chant the opening lines for him.

The rabbi agreed but did not call out the traditional Muslim words, "There is only one God and Muhammad is his prophet," as the mullah had asked. Instead he shouted out: "There is only one God and Moses is his prophet." In the streets around the minaret, bemused Muslims looked up at the top of the minaret and, when they spotted the grinning rabbi looking down on them in the streets below, they burst into good-natured laughter, realizing that he was teasing them.

In today's political climate, it is impossible to imagine such an expression of religious tolerance. It will take a significant shift to expand our spiritual, religious, and political horizons to see beyond the insular views that shape our perceptions of events, both personal and international. We await the day when the mullah invites the rabbi to the top of the minaret.

❖ ❖ ❖

DIFFERENT PEOPLES, ONE HUMANITY

Sometimes it is easy to forget that the ethnic violence we read about happening abroad is reliant on personal attitudes that we can find close to home. The following suggestions, points, and questions can be used to focus on your prevailing attitudes toward others.

1. Take time to read about the history of your country. Was it founded as a result of warfare? What happened to the people who lived on the land before it was settled by outsiders?

2. Look at the composition of the society you live in. If it is multicultural, is this reflected by the distribution of different ethnic groups in positions of influence? If not, does this bother you?

3. If you read about an influx of immigrants into your country do you feel acceptance or resentment? If you are happy with the idea, would that change if a refugee camp were set up near your home?

4. Do you enjoy coming across the food, dress, language, and other aspects of the culture of an ethnic group other than your own?

5. Realize that beneath the color of skin and diversity of languages and customs, we are all human beings, all faced with life's problems, and that we all need each other.

How should we react when we are faced with political oppression in our own countries, states, or regions? In the Bible Jesus was once asked whether Jews should pay tax to the Romans. His reply was that we should "render unto Caesar what is Caesar's, and render unto God what is God's." By this view, we have to concentrate on developing our spiritual lives and obey our inner voices, measuring our actions against the words of love, compassion, and kindness toward others that the great spiritual figures of the past have proclaimed. This is not always easy and can involve visible, nonviolent protest against political authority.

In September, 1997, I flew to Washington, D.C., to support the Buddhist monk, Venerable Maha Ghosananda, patriarch of Cambodia and thrice nominated for the Nobel Peace Prize, in his campaign against antipersonnel mines. While I was there I met a Cambodian named Pracha in a Buddhist monastery outside the city. Pracha had been sent by the Cambodian government to study engineering at an American university in the early 1970s, shortly before the Khmer Rouge, under the leadership of Pol Pot, organized its campaign throughout Cambodia to exterminate the educated masses and terrorize the uneducated. (During this terrible period Venerable Ghosananda and I lived as Buddhist monks in a monastery, a 15-hour drive south of Bangkok, Thailand. Venerable Ghosananda lost every member of his family—who were teachers, lawyers, diplomats.)

Pracha described to me a visit he made to his homeland some time after the massacres had taken place. He told me: "More than one-third of the population of Cambodia was murdered. They arrested educated people and took them to the local schools. In the classrooms, they systematically tortured people, clubbed them, or shot them day after day. The people in the villages could hear the screaming and terror in the schools."

It was a Buddhist holocaust. Hundreds of thousands died from poverty, sickness, and malnutrition, or were worked to death in the fields. The Khmer Rouge destroyed much of the cultural and religious life of Cambodia and destroyed many of the cities and villages.

With tears in his eyes, Pracha added: "When I arrived in the country I went to the village where so many members of my family died unspeakably cruel deaths. In Cambodia, it is normal to ask guests or family members when they arrive back home questions such as, 'Where have you come from today?' or 'Are you thirsty or hungry?' Instead, the first questions put to me were: 'How many relatives did you lose? How many relatives do you have left?'"

I asked Pracha what he felt today about the terror of the mid-1970s. He replied: "As Buddhists, we learn two things. One is not to cling to the past, as it will only fuel bitterness and hatred. We must be in the present and practice loving kindness toward everybody, including Pol Pot and the Khmer Rouge. It is never easy but we must learn to forgive and move on."

On the steps of the Senate later that day, the United Nations launched an international campaign to stop the production of land mines. Venerable Ghosananda said to the reporters and camera crew that we have to uproot the antipersonnel mines that exist in our hearts as well the mines planted in the ground. His words brought silence to the posse of reporters armed with pens, paper, tape recorders, and cameras.

What the Khmer Rouge did to Cambodia shows what can happen when political authority, backed by overwhelming armed force, assumes total control over a country. And the same tyranny is enacted at a personal level when our hearts have become as land mines. This inner defensiveness, of booby-trapping the terrain we wish to preserve as our own, can be caused by our desire for freedom—at the expense of the freedom of others.

As human beings, we have a special relationship to freedom, and we tend to do all in our power to protect it whenever circumstances threaten it. Our love of freedom runs deep in our being at the biological, social, and personal levels. History abounds with stories of quests for liberation, not only by individuals but by entire groups of people who felt oppressed by their situation—the exodus of the Israelites from Egypt being a famous paradigm in the West. In our love of freedom, we do not submit or surrender to demands.

But if, as a species, we yearn for the opportunity to live our lives free from subjugation, then we must apply the same moral principle to others. I want to live in peace. I want to feel accepted. Others want to feel accepted. We should remember that as individuals we can sacrifice our freedom by submitting to inner, unhealthy impulses and tendencies that make us unhappy, fearful, and intolerant. We can easily lose our freedom through bowing to the authority of others' demands or through conferring a misplaced sense of authority on our own problematic states of mind.

Our freedom also fades when we sell out through trying to satisfy our urges to get what we want as quickly as possible, even if it means walking over those who get in our way. At times, we give ourselves such self-importance that others want to keep away from us. And it is quite possible to drive ourselves crazy by pursuing the personal success on which our sense of self-worth hinges. This desire to feel important feeds our infatuation with celebrities, sports teams, charismatic leaders, and patriotic rallies. Through association, contact and loyalty, we experience the thrill of triumph over others. Our pleasure is bought at the expense of others.

So freedom, at heart, rests on our ability to think for ourselves, resisting (or overcoming) pressures from our inner urges and desires as well as compulsion from outside, especially during a national emergency. For it often happens that if a group of people are threatened, they are forced to come together in solidarity with each other. Previously, they may have disregarded their leader; now they rally around his or her words because of threats to their security. In this collective need for self-protection, we may whittle down the hard-won freedom to think for ourselves in the belief that conforming to the aims of our leaders will offer us more protection. Freedom is a natural instinct, but we abuse it if we use it as a justification to terrorize others.

❖ ❖ ❖

COUNTERING OPPRESSION

Political oppression is widespread throughout the world, more obvious and brutal in some places, more subtle and insidious in others. As individuals, what can we do to combat oppression both at a national and at a personal level? The following points of this "People's Peace Treaty" may serve to bolster our thoughts and actions in a positive way against oppression or its threat.

PEOPLE'S PEACE TREATY

1. I vow to dissociate myself completely from any destruction of life, including all acts of war, acts of terror, and executions. I will not support any declarations of war initiated by my country or any other that I support.

2. I vow not to attack or abuse other groups of people (nations, majorities, minorities, or individuals).

3. I vow to give support to organizations and groups working for peace, justice, political, economic, and environmental rights.

4. I vow to work to end suffering perpetuated through violence, fear, corruption, phobias, or greed.

5. I endeavor to persuade the military, arms manufacturers, and arms dealers to lay down their weapons and kill the hate inside themselves.

6. I vow to see people rather than the labels attached to people and to be aware of our common humanity.

7. I vow to work to end anger, aggression, or fear within myself as an expression of duty to humanity.

MEDITATION ON COMPASSION

Use this "Prayer of the Heart" as a meditation to overcome negative thoughts toward others and to instill in yourself feelings of loving-kindness for family, friends, neighbors, strangers, and enemies, both at home and abroad. By doing so you can help loosen the bonds that hold unjust authority in place.

PRAYER OF THE HEART

Let us keep our hearts focused.

Let me find kindness to negate resentment.

Let me show generosity to dissolve possessiveness.

Let me stand steady in the face of pain rather than live in fear.

Let me experience inquiry rather than reaction.

Let me be free from clinging and a narrow mind.

Let me express compassion rather than indifference.

So that my heart connects with the realities of others.

So that I stay true to an undying principle

Of treating others as I wish to be treated.

So awareness and respect pervade

My thoughts, words, and actions.

So that I live in a way that brings dignity and nobility to life

And reveals true freedom of being.

CHAPTER EIGHT

Coming to Terms
with Suffering

Blessed are the poor in spirit, for theirs is the kingdom of heaven,

Blessed are those who mourn, for they shall be comforted,

Blessed are the humble, for they shall inherit the earth ...

Blessed are the merciful, for they will be shown mercy,

Blessed are the pure in heart, for they will see God,

Blessed are the peacemakers, for they will be called sons of God.

Jesus of Nazareth
Matthew 5:3–5; 7–9

SUFFERING IS PART of the human condition. No matter how much we dislike or try to deny it, we are subject to suffering. The great challenge from a spiritual perspective is how to react to it, to come to terms with it. In Buddhism the fact of suffering is emphasized in the Buddha's Four Noble Truths. These state that suffering is part of being human; suffering has its root cause in our desires and in the desires of others; it is possible for suffering to end; and there is an "Eightfold Path" that enables us to end suffering (it consists of right view, right intention, right speech, right action, right livelihood, right effort, right mindfulness, and right meditation).

Throughout this book the intention has been to explore and suggest ways of dealing with different types of suffering and its causes and effects. In the first three chapters we looked at grief, at dealing with our responses to conflict, and how to work with anger. Chapter 4 led us into thinking about how to cope with the inevitability of death and Chapter 5 into thinking about stereotypes and prejudices and the way they condition our responses. In the preceding two chapters we examined what it means to be truly intimate with life and explored the nature of authority and how to face up to its abuse. This chapter gives an overview of conflict and suffering and what we can do to achieve authentic freedom from them.

THE PATH TO AWARENESS

As a species on this earth, we have a remarkable capacity to develop our full potential as human beings. But to do so requires us to refocus our lives and be willing to move our consciousness into the unknown. This is a tremendous undertaking, since it forces us to question numerous things about ourselves that we may have taken for granted. Some spiritual teachers warn us not to sleepwalk through life. So, it is a truly significant step if we can resolve to wake up and start our lives all over again—to feel that we have been born anew into this strange, wonderful, and unfathomable world.

As this book has pointed out in various ways, we have to stop clinging to the past if we are to forge ahead into new levels of human consciousness and vision. The steps we take will certainly go against the effort we may have put into being successful in our consumer culture. It takes boldness to ask ourselves probing questions and then to live with those questions. But by doing so, we will develop a deeper and broader interest in life, a process we can help through increasing our spiritual knowledge and experience, by traveling, meditating, exposing ourselves to nature, and making contact with the wise.

In a way, this spiritual journey might be described as an adventure in consciousness that knows neither limit nor end. This adventure gives access to a love and happiness that will mean more to us than any other kind of experience. It does not matter how difficult the spiritual path is, or how often it seems our progress is matched by temporary retreat. The path requires an inner statement of deep commitment.

Not surprisingly, we may not know where to begin our journey or, if we have already begun it, where the next steps lead to. In the spiritual arena, there has been in recent years a huge explosion of activities, practices, religions, and beliefs. Despite the bewildering number of teachings, courses, workshops, and retreats now available and the difficulty in choosing among them, many of them will help us cultivate a deep spiritual sensitivity toward life, resolve the suffering centered around the activities of the self, and unveil a liberated awareness.

It is not easy to determine what is of value in the spiritual supermarket. But I regard it as a noble pursuit and way of life that we at least try to achieve a different consciousness and through it find some kind of understanding about the deep questions of existence. With the sheer diversity of approaches, we must constantly bear in mind what our spiritual goal is. And we should remember what the old mystics have told us, namely that every step we take toward God invites him to take a step toward us, and every step along the spiritual path brings the end or fulfillment of the spiritual path that much closer.

In the light of awareness, we do not have to stick rigidly to a set of beliefs or a range of eclectic views. We simply have to explore ways of rising above the problems of the world and at the same time express love and compassion for those suffering in the mire of daily existence. If our exploration is successful, we will find that our quest-awakened consciousness embraces three crucial factors:

1. The ethic that demands we treat others as we wish to be treated.

2. The mindfulness and meditation to explore existence with our whole being, moment to moment.

3. The realization of an indestructible liberation that is manifested as an unstoppable friendship toward life.

It is not easy to embrace these three points. But if we settle for anything else, we end up with the finite and limited. Spiritual teachings point to that which is infinite and limitless. If we can grasp this, we can make sense of terror and the obscene events that torment our lives. For we then realize that they, too, belong to the fullness of things—whether we like it or not. Also, having a spiritual conception of the human race as a family means that we will probably feel deeply uncomfortable about acts of war or terror committed in our name. We will have the sense that the machinery of war can never be the answer to acts of violence or intense human conflict between people.

From a spiritual standpoint, we may feel hemmed in. On the one hand, we do not wish to condone more bloodshed to answer terror, but on the other hand we do not have the answer. The spiritual life calls upon us to stay steady with the truth of this experience rather than revert to a simplistic stance of "we have to do something"—which often means sending in the military. It takes a certain strength to keep the questioning alive, so that from it we can resist the way of conflict and forge a different, more enlightened relationship with the rest of the human family.

It is a profound act to look into the here and now and care so deeply for events that it keeps alive our resolve to express a noble response, rather than submit to the demands of the few, or the many, who fire themselves

SPIRITUAL PRACTICE

By engaging in spiritual practice we not only transform ourselves but also, in doing so, become better able to serve the world at large. This practice is essentially an active, dynamic pursuit that we can follow alone or with others. The following points set out some of its characteristics and benefits.

• Through practice we can set ourselves free from destructive thoughts and habits and careless actions.

• Practice enables us to free our minds from greed, hate, and fear.

• Through practice we can cultivate awareness and reach new depths of meditation. We can also gain spiritual insights into the nature of things.

• Through practice we become willing to challenge abuses of power and can influence the world accordingly, for practice includes the political realm as much as it does the the social and religious spheres.

• Practice helps us to rise to the various challenges of life and to see that it is relevant to all experiences and situations. Also, struggle may be an essential part of practice.

• Without practice, theorizing about things can become an irresponsible activity. Without the use of reason, practice leads nowhere. Practice involves awareness, experience, and application.

• In practice, we can awaken intuitive knowledge and use it purposefully for the welfare of all.

• Through practice we can translate our living perceptions into resolute awareness, compassionate action, and transcendent vision.

up whenever a major conflict arises. The spiritual path is full of heart, full of hope, and requires the fearless determination of men and women to point the way to a different kind of world, where we do everything in our power to show our love for others, regardless of the way we are told to view events. We must never forget that it is a precious matter for a human being to think differently and respond differently to terror. In the spiritual life, we believe in the power of love, fearless compassion, and constructive engagement to resolve suffering.

BECOMING A SPIRITUAL WARRIOR

In Yangon, the capital of Myanmar (formerly Burma), the Nobel Peace Prize winner Aung San Suu Kyi remains firm and unflinching as the voice of her people. While the rest of the world takes little interest in Myanmar, since it has no strategic importance, the "Mother of the Nation" stays present in her country 24 hours a day, 365 days a year. Even when her British husband was dying from cancer in Oxford, England, she stayed in Myanmar. For if she left, the oppressive military regime would never allow her back into her homeland. Aung San Suu Kyi is a spiritual warrior.

Contrary to popular opinion, spiritual practitioners need not lead meek and submissive lives, spending many hours every day in prayer and meditation, though that may be a priority at times. The true practitioners are willing to go to war. As spiritual warriors they do not fight to destroy the lives and habitats of men, women, and children; they make war on greed, hate, and fear, inwardly and outwardly. In the spiritual life, there is often a great deal of emphasis on working on oneself first before daring to venture to help others: spiritual warriors are concerned with inner and outer situations equally.

Some people just drift along in life, mixing consumer with spiritual values. The spiritual warrior sees things differently. For such a person knows that he or she is already part of the world and makes war on unhealthy states of mind whenever they arise. One of the features of the warrior is the willingness to take risks, to uphold values that go against the mainstream of thinking, or to go into areas of risk or danger. The warrior is brave but can also be foolhardy; courageous but at times afraid; strong but vulnerable. At times, warriors have to rely on their inner intentions to work for change, to resolve suffering, not increase it.

For most of us, the struggle to reinforce the ego and to get our own way means we remain in conflict with others. If we wish to progress to a new level of understanding, we must try to break free from fixing our consciousness in either a hostile or suppliant mode. We become spiritual warriors through being wise and engaging with the unthinkable. In doing so we dissolve the boundary that divides us from others until there is genuine contact between us. In dealing with conflict, we enter the heart of a situation until we feel we are in a crucible producing inner strength and fearlessness.

The warrior, therefore, has little appetite for passivity, simplistic kindness, and staying inwardly calm while ignoring the existence of suffering in others, at home or abroad. Both in Buddhism and the world of psychotherapy, there are far too many voices who settle for inner calm and a noncritical attitude, rather than extolling the fearlessness that is needed to transform the most painful of situations.

As warriors, we can rise to the challenge of championing the rights of others through noble intentions and action. We make ourselves willing to endure the sufferings of outrageous misfortune and apparent defeats and ridicule by trusting that the spirit for real change will triumph over the terror inflicted upon others.

This vision and outlook marks the spiritual warrior from politicians and religious leaders who advocate "just wars." As warriors, we pay respect to our enemies, no matter how ill-conceived and hate-filled their actions. We view violence—no matter how obscene—as a nightmare not only for those who suffer, but also for those who inflict it.

As warriors, we must remain fully aware of how much cruelty, ruthlessness, and pain some people will deliberately inflict upon others. It will take every drop of our energy to sustain our determination to

THE SOLDIER VERSUS THE WARRIOR

To be a spiritual warrior it is important to realize that, rather than depend on force of arms, we have to rely on our inner intentions to work for change and to resolve suffering. This constitutes a crucial difference between the warrior and the soldier. Other distinctions to bear in mind are:

- The soldier will kill.
- The warrior will work to transform.

- The soldier will follow his commander.
- The warrior has nobody to rely upon.

- The soldier may put his trust in God.
- The spiritual warrior may not know what God is.

act creatively and persistently to turn a horrendous situation around through the power of the mind, the application of language, and compassionate engagement. The old retaliatory ways will have to take second place to fresh beginnings, free from any position supported by an undercurrent of hate.

We can embrace this dynamic process of transformation by being willing to jettison aggressive views and habitual ways of reacting to what we hear or believe. Such a radical change can only take place today, not tomorrow, next week, or next year.

ACHIEVING AUTHENTIC FREEDOM

There is something rather sad about letting our lives become an instrument of society. We follow its dictates and allow relentless propaganda to mold us to its demands. Many of us in the West have made a mantra out of the word "freedom" as we shout it from the rooftops for the rest of the world to hear. In so doing, we have murdered the meaning of "freedom." For while we broadcast the freedom that we enjoy and wish to promote, we easily forget that all the while we ourselves are restricted by inner and outer compulsions—by our anger and greed, for example, or by the dictates of market forces, which may land us with debts, worries, and a deep spiritual vacuum.

If, instead of going on about freedom, we acknowledged our shortcomings as a society, we could learn from other societies and perhaps they, in response, might wish to learn from us. But this would take awareness, humility, and wisdom from all parties to get to the heart of the matter.

At a personal level, to achieve authentic freedom we need to examine ourselves and be willing to learn from others. Compelled to live lives of various routines and patterns, we feel totally at a loss when they grind to a halt. If we split up with a partner, we may rush headlong into another relationship that repeats the errors of the preceding one. On losing a job, we fail to take the opportunity to change our lives but watch as the old patterns are reborn so that all we can think about is getting a new job. In the old and the familiar, we feel safe.

Our daily lives can be sustained indefinitely with a certain mediocrity; but sometimes we may feel that we are caught in a dreary rut in comparison with those who seem to have grasped the adventure of life. We wonder sometimes how other people not only take risks to live a free and different way of life but are also willing to endure horrendous conditions without regret or fear. When we compare ourselves to such people, we often let feelings of competitiveness, desire, and envy get the better of us. But we should hold them up as models, and let them shake us out of any complacency.

It is impossible to achieve authentic freedom without taking risks, and it is notable that explorers and mountaineers often describe their feelings of freedom and serenity in the midst of potential danger. On January 19, 1915, Ernest Shackleton, the British Antarctic explorer, and 27 men prepared to abandon their 300-ton wooden ship, the *Endurance*, when ice froze around it. The ship had zigzagged for a thousand miles trying to break free from the ice floe. Eventually, the crew abandoned the paralyzed ship and tried to haul their supplies over the ice ridges until they found land. They spent five months living on the floating ice, waiting for it to melt and break up in the spring.

Camped on the ice, the captain of the ship, Frank Worsley, wrote in his diary: "While looking ahead, and planning to meet all possible dangers, I do not worry about these dangers, which will probably be very great, but live comfortably and happy in the present, and can truly say that at present I am enjoying myself far more than I would in civilization."

Six of the crew, including Shackleton and Worsley, then rowed a staggering 800 miles in a small boat in gale-swept seas to get help for the rest of the men, who were then dangerously camped on a small, uninhabited island. The men waited there for four months until Shackleton found a ship to cut through the ice to reach them. They all survived.

It is hard to imagine the conditions these men put up with month after month. Their world seems far removed from our daily activities—few would wish to rush off to sit on an ice floe in a desperate state of uncertainty for months on end. However, the example of Frank Worsley should encourage us that by living in the present, taking each day, each moment, as it comes, we can transcend even the most pressing problems and conditions. Life is shorter than a flash of lightning across the night sky. Sometimes we need to take a long, hard look at our own lives and dare to step out onto the cold ice of existence. By doing so, by taking risks, we can free ourselves from the bleakness of our unchallenging lives and begin to tackle the prejudices, anger, and desires that constrict us.

If we make an inner shift that reaches down to the root of our being, we find that freedom of expression matters more than the pursuit of comfort. Through courage and determination—as Worsley's account reminds us— we can endure the most challenging of circumstances. Freedom first, security second— this should be our thinking. For centuries, the Muslim community has remembered the truth of this through their proverb: "Trust in Allah but don't forget to tie your camel."

FREEDOM TO CHANGE

Are you ready to change your way of life, with all of its anguish and disappointment, to a life that transcends suffering and pain? This change, this transformation, would really say something about your capacity to experience authentic freedom. So, if you can, do it. Here are some questions that might help you on your way.

• Are you free to change yourself, outwardly and inwardly?
• Are you free to move on from being a cog in a machine, whether in your job or in another sphere of life?
• Are you free to wake up daily without layers of dissatisfaction running through the day?
• Are you free to act unselfishly and be generous to others, whether friends, family, or strangers?
• Are you free to love much and want little?
• Are you free to live a liberated life, not bound to daily enslavement to a cause or a position?
• Are you free to take risks, to explore unconventional avenues of experience and service to others?

To make a fundamental transition in our values, we have to learn to think our own thoughts rather than repeat with unquestioning obedience the thoughts of others. We may blurt out unexamined, superficial comments in response to trivial situations, but it is different when it comes to expressing a position about suffering and its resolution. In this case, we must develop the capacity to give all forms of life the dignity and respect they deserve. That means taking risks for the direct welfare of others.

We need to be able to think for ourselves; we need to meditate on fresh ways of bringing about immediate and radical changes. We need to be determined to dig deep into reality and go beyond initial, simplistic conclusions we may have had, based on little knowledge. In the unknown, in a state of inner emptiness, we have the potential to look at any problem, no matter how terrifying it appears. In the depth of such exploration, the following are five areas for reflection:

1 | ARE WE REPEATING WHAT WE HAVE HEARD ELSEWHERE?

We should not underestimate our capacity to take up a view just because it "sounds right." Being fixed on a certain line of argument, we repeat it every time the relevant topic arises. This blind support for something makes its impact on our minds, speech, and activities: our narrow fixation around the idea strengthens the notion of self, of "I" and "my," as if what we claim to be true has its roots in the depths of insight.

We may also have the tendency to grasp ideas from a variety of sources and make them our own. The ego invests in these adopted views to bolster itself; then we (or our egos) assert ourselves through claiming to know the way things really are. This deception creeps in, fooling us and others, often ending up adding to the stockpile of suffering in the world.

2 | HAVE I THOUGHT THROUGH WHAT I AM SAYING?

This question is about reflecting on the various aspects of suffering and its causes. A truly conscious approach remains open to exploration and takes into account the time required for reflection and study. Having a one-sided view generally derives from the simplistic notion that only one cause is responsible for some tragic event.

Our immediate response to being harmed is usually along the lines of: "You have hurt me. What you did caused me pain." However, we could go deeper into the circumstances and ask: "What caused you to hurt me? Do I have any responsibility? What do you feel is unresolved? Is there anything that I can do that will make a difference? What were some of the conditions you drew upon for this position to come about?" The willingness to look beyond a simplistic response will result in a balanced perception that can help resolve a problem.

3 | DO YOU HAVE A WIDE KNOWLEDGE OF THE SUBJECT?

We need to have a genuine interest in the subjects we reflect on. This takes more effort than reading the newspaper or watching the news. We have to go further and investigate for ourselves the nature of suffering, its causes, its resolution, and the means to achieve this. This includes reading books, watching documentaries, discussing, reflecting, doing practical exercises, and probing deeply. We also need to listen to others while making sure we do not lose our central aim of resolving suffering, no matter how intense it is. Our determination on this point will safeguard us from getting lost in obscure details or pursuing knowledge for its own sake.

4 | ARE YOU ABLE TO TAKE AN OVERVIEW?

Deep inquiry also requires breadth, so we should have an overall perception of things and events and be able to place suffering in the context of the universal human condition. We know the world as much from being on the outside as being within it. This means we remain firmly in the world, using love and action to resolve suffering, but not being so attached to the world that we cause harm and sorrow. This way we can value living in relationship with others with mutual respect and trust. Unless we develop the capacity to transcend the world of mutual torment and take an overview, we will live a blinkered existence, unable to see further than our ideas and the ideas of those who disagree with us.

5 | DO YOU REALIZE THAT INSIGHT AFFECTS THE VIEWPOINT?

When an idea has become fixed in our minds, it can play havoc in the world through our constant determination to impose it on others. This implies we think that other people's ideas count for little and that our own ideas are the reason for existence. Certain that its view of reality is correct, the conceited self becomes cemented into such a rigid position that it obscures the real world, which becomes a backdrop for the idea's propagation. However, by welcoming fresh knowledge and new insights, and paying attention to the present moment, we can develop to the point when we can express an understanding born of a deep connection with life.

LIBERATING OUR CONSCIOUSNESS

The final entry in Etty Hillesum's diary, written in her flat at 6 Gabriel Metustraat in Amsterdam on Saturday, June 14, 1942, read: "I have tried to look that 'suffering' of mankind fairly and squarely in the face. I have fought it out, or rather, something inside me has fought it out, and suddenly there were answers to many desperate questions. All was smooth going after a short but violent battle from which I emerged just a fraction more mature. All one can hope to do is to keep oneself humbly available, to allow oneself to be a battlefield.

"After all, the problems must be accommodated, have somewhere to struggle and come to rest. We, poor humans, must put our inner space at their service and not run away."

Etty Hillesum died in the Auschwitz concentration camp on November 30, 1943.

Hillesum's determination to confront life head on and put her "inner space" at the service of problems is a poignant and inspiring rallying cry for us to mount the effort needed to transform terror and suffering—and in doing so attempt to liberate our consciousness. And this applies not only to problems and suffering that occur through extraordinary events but also those of everyday life, which are often compounded by our rigid way of thinking and confused states of mind.

Our attitude toward life is all important. It becomes pernicious when it is beset by various competing ideas. By refusing to cling to any one idea, we can discover awareness, love, and freedom, which reveal themselves through our actions. Otherwise, we live in an emotional and intellectual prison that prevents our spiritual values becoming manifest in our everyday lives. In our consumer society, it is easy to become infatuated by the world of language, names, and concepts: we can become mesmerized with thoughts and words—as though language revealed the ultimate truth of things. In many respects, it is a dream world, a phantom, an empty formation acting as a veil drawn across the immediate present.

We believe in the idea of nations and regions, east and west, here and there, as though these "divisions" truly existed. We perceive the world from the narrow position of the self rather than from pure awareness, which functions like a mirror, revealing all that arises and passes impartially. Ultimately, nations, regions, and groups are forms of separation the self has constructed. A deep response to existence emerges only when the self drops away from being the central reference point. Then the indivisible truth reveals itself.

To find this truth we often have to struggle with our negative habits. Even in the midst of affluence, we wage war on ourselves—for example, we abuse our bodies and minds through smoking, drinking, and drugs. We can distract our lives by madly pursuing self-gratification while becoming indifferent to the suffering of others, near or far. There is little meaning to such a way of life. It is surely better to live with wisdom and compassion for a single day than abide for decades at the mercy of our latent tendencies toward narrow self-interest. In our society, we often read magazine interviews in which the rich and famous reveal their problems and unhappiness. In the light of real terror and the suffering it brings, these complaints seem petty, as do the trivial pursuits that many of us engage in. We must break free from what are really purposeless priorities and express our humanity, our generosity of spirit.

To transform terror we must keep alive the end of liberating our consciousness from its perilous condition—a state of being that wastes our lives on this earth and exploits its resources. We have to keep the inner voice of protest alive and well against exploitation by profit-driven forces within our society. Equally, we must protest against inflicting harm on others in the guise of self-preservation. We must be willing to sustain compassionate convictions, to ensure that the heart stays steady in its values so that nothing destroys the power of love.

We need inspiration. We need to seek contact with those who live lives of love and freedom. Listen to them. Meet them. Spend time in their company. Learn from them. If we cannot find such people in the present, then we must turn to the past, to men and women who placed freedom before all else. We need to hear and read about these great souls of the world. We need to remember their words and act upon them in our own humble way. They inspire us because they faced the depths of terror and realized its emptiness.

One such soul was Marie Kuderikova. On March 26, 1943, Marie, aged 22, wrote a letter to her parents from a prison for political prisoners in Breslau, Poland, after being betrayed for working for an illegal organization. Two days after she wrote the letter, the Gestapo executed her. "Today, the twenty-sixth of March, 1943, two days after having reached the twenty-second year of my life, I shall draw my last breath. I have always had the courage to live—moreover I am not losing it in the face of what in human speech is called death. I should like to take upon myself all your sorrow and pain.

"Today is a beautiful day. Do you feel as I do that fragrance, that loveliness? The naked nerve of the soul was stirred by the poetry of the commonplace, the smell of boiled potatoes, smoke and the clatter of spoons, birds, sky, being alive—the everyday pulse beat of life. Love it, love one another, learn love, defend love, spread love. So that you may perceive the beauty of the obvious gift of life as I do—that is my wish for myself. So that you may be able to give and receive. I am not afraid of what is coming. I have felt the urge to the good, the sublime, the human. My whole life has been beautiful."

Marie Kuderikova faced what is for most of us the ultimate terror: extinction. And she faced it unflinchingly. She had been blessed with "the courage to live" and with the ability to transform the grimness of Breslau and her prospects there into a radiant vision in which the small things of life, the everyday details, are charged with significance. Her example is there for us to draw on. By facing terror we can understand it; and in understanding it we can change it from something that inspires in us feelings of anger, hate, and revenge to something that can help us to heal divisions, to become fully human, to achieve a state of being free, loved, and understood.

MEDITATION ON COMPASSION

For the final meditation of the book it seems appropriate to concentrate on its core message: that love and compassion can transform our own and others' suffering. Read these lines aloud or silently, dwelling on the idea that a personal commitment to compassion, no matter how small or inadequate, can send out ripples of light.

- I do not have to look very far to see suffering in this world.
- I know that pity is not the same as compassion.
- Compassion calls me to respond, to make sacrifice.
- Compassion demands something from my concern.
- I cannot ignore what I know.
- I can only respond as courageously as possible.
- I can offer even though it is hard.
- I can share even though I resist.
- I can express something that reveals I am awake.
- I know that my gestures for others seem like nothing compared to the suffering in the world.
- Yet, I act anyway,

Never expecting anything in return
Knowing that it is a small token.

- But these gestures of love

Regularly expressed reveal my humanity
Reminding me, we all stand connected
In this web of life together.

ACKNOWLEDGMENTS

I WISH TO express my deepest gratitude to the men and women around the world who work tirelessly to transform suffering so that people can live with joy and dignity. I regard service to others as the noblest form of human activity. The accounts of people's struggles through their pain provide all of us with insight and inspiration. I have had the privilege of listening and responding to stories of people's lives in many parts of the world. People, young and old alike, share this remarkable capacity of the human spirit to pass with dignity through the most difficult and distressing of circumstances.

The teachings of the Buddha continue to be a core influence in my writing. I wish to acknowledge the work of Rawda Basir in Nablus, Palestine, and Stephen Fulder in Clil, Israel, for their efforts to secure peace, justice, and reconciliation between the two communities. I have appreciated the Middle East news reports from Robert Fisk of the Independent newspaper, London, for his deep concerns for ordinary people whose lives become tormented through political decisions.

I would like to thank all those involved in the production of this book, in particular Cathy Meeus and James Harper. I wish to thank Debbie Thorpe of Godsfield Press, UK, for inviting me to write a book that addresses intense suffering from a spiritual perspective. I also wish to thank Brenda Rosen, who kindly edited the original comprehensive proposal for the book. Many thanks also to Gill Farrer-Halls for her finely attuned editing skills and practical advice on writing during the past ten years.

I wish to thank Nina Wedborn from Stockholm for her helpful suggestions for this book and my daughter, Nshorna Titmuss, for her secretarial assistance. Much appreciation to Hans Gruber and Anne Ashton for their support and service to the Dharma.

Finally, I wish to thank all those men and women who dedicate their lives to expressing wisdom and compassion in the face of terror. We cannot repay our debt of gratitude to such people.